ENDING
THE WAR IN
IRAQ

ENDING
THE WAR IN
IRAQ

Tom Hayden

AKASHIC BOOKS
NEW YORK

Published by Akashic Books
©2007 Tom Hayden

ISBN-13: 978-1-933354-45-3
Library of Congress Control Number: 2007926047
All rights reserved
Printed in Canada

First printing

Akashic Books
PO Box 1456
New York, NY 10009
info@akashicbooks.com
www.akashicbooks.com

Acknowledgments

I wish to thank the crew at Akashic Books—publisher Johnny Temple, Ibrahim Ahmad, Johanna Ingalls, and Aaron Petrovich—whose vision, commitment, and energy were crucial in making this book possible.

I wish to acknowledge the suffering of the Iraqi people, which has forced a rethinking of American purpose and foreign policy; and the needless, wasteful suffering of thousands of American soldiers.

Thanks to the global peace movement, whose moral pressure is weakening the pillars of the Machiavellian state.

There are no happy endings to war. Nothing can justify the horrors of the present one, but hopefully lessons are being learned. As Robert F. Kennedy said on the night of Martin Luther King Jr.'s death, quoting Aeschylus, "In our sleep, pain which cannot forget falls drop by drop upon the heart until, in our own despair, against our will, comes wisdom through the awful grace of God."

TABLE OF CONTENTS

INTRODUCTION

O n January 27, 2007, I looked at the U.S. Capitol surrounded by a sea of antiwar protesters massing to march once again. I stood on the same spot fortytwo years before, in April 1965, at the first national march against the Vietnam War. Then, as now, a president was violating a voter mandate for peace. Lyndon Johnson had indicated during his presidential campaign in 1964 that he would not send young American soldiers to Southeast Asia. Because of that promise, young radicals like myself decided on the slogan, *Part of the way with LBJ*, knowing that the alternative was the conservative Barry Goldwater. Johnson betrayed his vow, however, escalating the conflict to a ground war by 1965. Our march grew accordingly, reaching 25,000—said at that time to be the largest antiwar outpouring in memory. Little did I understand that we would be marching for a decade. We marched largely against the wishes of our elders. Leaders of both parties claimed we were soft on Communism.

Similarly, in 2007, President George W. Bush betrayed the voter mandate of the previous autumn, when ending the war in Iraq was the primary reason that American voters had deposed a Republican congressional majority. Despite this clear ultimatum, and the advice of many conservatives, Bush authorized sending at least 21,500 more American troops into a war that most observers believed was unwinnable.[1] In addition, he

---

[1] See, for example, David S. Cloud and Michael R. Gordon, "General Seeking High Troop Level for Iraq into '08," *New York Times*, March 8, 2007: "When the Bush Administration announced its troop buildup in January, it said it was

pushed to the brink of expanding the war to Iran. But in deploying more troops to Iraq, Bush also triggered a new wave of protest energy.

The crowd before me was one of the largest I'd seen in forty years of marching on Washington. Though the *Washington Post* reported that the numbers fell short of the organizers' expectations,[2] and though the mainstream media settled on an arbitrary figure of "tens of thousands," my experienced instincts told me that closer to a half-million Americans were encircling the Capitol. A crisis was in the air, as the White House had failed in Iraq and at home. The war was poisoning our civic life, filling our graveyards and veterans' hospitals, denying funds for domestic needs, isolating our country, and destroying our nation's reputation.

I was recovering from heart surgery at the beginning of the war, but remember being hooked on the television accounts by a passion awakened from my past. Sensing one fabrication after another, I sank into despair at the media's collaboration, but believed from the first days that the occupation would bring forward a resistance. I began blogging, trying to reveal the story between the lines. Since early 2003, nearly one hundred of those blogs and essays have appeared online, in the *Nation*, *Huffington Post*, *In These Times*, and the op-ed pages of the *Los Angeles Times* and *San Francisco Chronicle*. My audience included both the older and newer antiwar movements, as I attempted to apply my experience from the 1960s to this rapidly unfolding conflict. While criticism of the war increased, I found myself not only writing and marching, but meeting with mem-

sending 21,500 troops to Baghdad and Anbar Province. Since then the Pentagon has said that as many as 7,000 additional support troops would also be deployed, including some 2,200 additional military police . . . These increases would bring the total number of American troops in Iraq to around 160,000."
[2] Michael Ruane and Frederick Kunkle, "Thousands Protest Bush Policy," *Washington Post*, January 28, 2007.

bers of Congress and the political establishment to try to avert a deepening quagmire. I traveled on several occasions to Amman, Jordan, and London to interview scores of displaced Iraqis living in exile. I now teach a sociology course on Iraq at Pitzer College in the Claremont Colleges complex east of Los Angeles, and am committed to chronicling another war and another antiwar movement until the end, which may be a long time from now. Or not so long; it depends partly on what Americans do.

I believe there is a growing convergence between the events in Iraq and those here at home. Polls show that the Iraqi people overwhelmingly favor a timetable for withdrawing American troops, combined with continued assistance in reconstructing their broken country. A large majority even favors armed attacks on U.S. forces as a right of national resistance. At least 131 members of the Iraqi Parliament, nearly half the body, have petitioned for the U.S. to withdraw, and the number is growing.[3] The same parliament's National Sovereignty Committee has unanimously called for a withdrawal timetable (see Chapter 3). Most Iraqis are at odds with the sectarian, American-backed executive clique currently in power in Baghdad.

If the Iraqi regime was not so tightly rigged at the top, the parliament itself would give us the boot (but politely, perhaps with red carpets). Iraqi voices for withdrawal are seldom referenced in the mainstream American media. Neither is the grotesque mismanagement of the Baghdad regime itself. Occasionally the media mentions that the oil ministry is "rife with corruption." Several authors have documented the dishonest practices of American contractors, but few have zeroed in on the heart of the regime itself.

[3] Sudarsan Raghavan, "Shiite Clerics' Rivalry Deepens in Fragile Iraq," *Washington Post*, December 21, 2006.

For example, the current president of Iraq is Jalal Tala-bani, who has been a Kurdish leader for decades. Like other American-backed victors, he inhabits a mansion previously belonging to Saddam Hussein's family. Talabani brags that the Kurdish town of Sulaimaniya now has twenty billionaires and 2,000 millionaires, that he spends an estimated half-million dollars for a week's hotel stay in Paris, and that he receives up to $1 million per month in discretionary funds; he has sup-posedly handed out envelopes containing fifty crisp $100 bills to journalists and associates.[4] These self-aggrandizing patterns are almost never reported, and when they are, they are usually presented as lifestyle foibles.

Despite the national differences, many Americans are coming to conclusions about the war that are similar to those of most Iraqis. As of this writing, roughly thirty per-cent of the U.S. want our troops home now, about sixty percent want a timetable for their speedy withdrawal, and a Democrat-led Congress has a mandate for peace and an end to government corruption. In late 2005, nearly half of all Americans wanted to consider impeaching the presi-dent.[5] Support for Bush and his Iraq policies has dropped below thirty percent. Yet the Bush Administration and in-fluential contractors like Halliburton and Blackwater USA continue to prevent the inevitable withdrawal of American forces. The precise U.S. and Iraqi casualty rates, as well as the actual costs of the war, are deliberately hidden from the American people. Billions of tax dollars disappear through the sieve of unaccountable special interests. The deception and corruption practiced by the White House extends from the Beltway to Baghdad, with U.S. National Security Advis-er Stephen J. Hadley writing memos suggesting "monetary

---

[4] Jon Lee Anderson, "Mr. Big," *New Yorker*, February 5, 2007.
[5] Ispos Public Affairs poll, October 6–9, 2005.

support" for Iraqi parties that follow America's lead in Green Zone politics.[6]

The point is that strong majorities in both countries want American troops returned home and feel disenfranchised by their governments. This consensus prevails despite legitimate worries about healing the deep wounds of postwar Iraq. Either the Iraqis, free from U.S. pressure, need to install a new transitional governing circle in Baghdad—one whose spirit is consistent with that of the Iraqi people—or the American public has to elect new leadership in Washington in 2008.

Just as the path into Iraq was blurred by fabrications, so is the way out. It is commonly asserted that American troops will be able to "stand down" only when Iraqis "stand up." But that won't happen, at least not in the foreseeable future. Whatever the original intentions, the U.S. has raised a Frankenstein monster in Iraq—a country ruled by a Shi'a and Kurdish alliance of convenience engaged in a vendetta against their former Sunni Arab rulers, whose people are being ethnically cleansed from many parts of the country. As these pages will demonstrate, Iraq's repressive government is replete with sectarian militias, some trained in Iran, dominating a brutal interior ministry and essential state organs. The fate of Iraqi women, once a purported American concern, is long forgotten amidst rampant sexual violence and strict interpretations of Shari'a law.[7] An insurgency, at first mostly

---

[6] See transcript of leaked memo by Stephen J. Hadley, "Text of the National Security Adviser's Memorandum on the Political Situation in Iraq," *New York Times*, November 29, 2006. The CIA and State Department spend millions on influencing internal Iraqi politics, but their operations are rarely, if ever, mentioned. The 1998 Iraq Liberation Act, signed by President Clinton, allocated $97 million for regime change in Baghdad. At least $33 million went to Ahmed Chalabi's Iraqi National Congress to subsidize sham operations in Iraq, buy fleets of luxury cars, and manipulate the American media and Congress into accepting the WMD thesis. See Michael Isikoff and David Corn, *Hubris: The Inside Story of Spin, Scandal, and the Selling of the Iraq War* (Crown, 2006), p. 50.
[7] Amy Goodman, *Democracy Now!*, March 6, 2007.

Sunni in composition, appears to be gaining traction across sectarian lines. Iraq is a failed state that can no longer provide basic security to its inhabitants. Thus, making a future U.S. withdrawal dependent on the current regime in Baghdad will turn all Americans into prisoners of a perpetual war.

Even worse, the White House is reversing its definition of allies and enemies in mid-course. In 2003, the foe was a "WMD-armed" Saddam Hussein and his Sunni-dominated Ba'ath Party, and shortly after the fall of the regime, it became the "Sunni-led" insurgency. By 2007, the U.S. seemed to be changing direction again, deciding that the greatest danger is Iran, a Shi'a state which benefits from the very regime the U.S. has empowered in Baghdad. The U.S. is now warning Iran to stop meddling in Iraq, despite the fact that Iran supports the same Shi'a Iraqi government as the U.S. On the other hand, the U.S. continues to back Saudi Arabia, which provides funding, volunteers, and diplomatic muscle to the Sunni insurgency. As Martin Indyk, a former State Department official and the current director of the Saban Center for Middle East Policy at the Brookings Institution said in 2007, "This could get very complicated. Everything is upside down."[8]

There is an imperial logic in this topsy-turvy policy, however, that exploits fissures between Muslims to ensure U.S. military and strategic dominance over a divided Middle East. To imagine U.S. policy more clearly, picture a giant oil tanker with a crew of four—George W. Bush, Dick Cheney, Condoleezza Rice, and outgoing Ambassador Zalmay Khalilzad—all affiliated with Big Oil, navigating a narrow strait amidst violent sectarian waves churned up by its very presence.[9]

[8] Seymour Hersh, "The Redirection," New Yorker, March 5, 2007.
[9] The relation of Bush and Cheney to the oil industry is well known. Chevron once named an oil tanker after Rice, who served on the company's board. Khalilzad was a paid consultant to Unocal in Afghanistan, where he supported the Taliban as a force that could be worked with. See Jon Lee Anderson, "American Viceroy: Zalmay Khalilzad's Mission," New Yorker, December 19, 2005.

It is difficult, as I have learned in the past, to write about historic events before they are over. A number of useful books have recently appeared, most of them diagnosing the profound manipulation and mismanagement woven into the invasion period of 2002–2003. Several have singled out neo-conservatives or the so-called "Vulcans" of the war cabinet for special blame. But despite having documented and denounced the flawed grounds for invading Iraq, few of these critics have recommended a decision to withdraw. Given the fallout from the original mistake, they now suggest that it would be even worse to exit Iraq. For example, in a devastating critique called *Blind into Baghdad* in which he exposes the Iraqi army as being virtually nonexistent, James Fallows nevertheless writes:

> *I have come to this sobering conclusion: The United States can best train Iraqis, and therefore best help itself leave Iraq, only by making very long-term commitments to stay.*[10]

Making the same argument—that it was a mistake to invade but would be a bigger mistake to leave—the 2006 *Iraq Study Group Report* finds that the U.S.-created Iraqi government and army are dysfunctional and fraught with sectarian strife, then proposes the withdrawal only of U.S. combat troops in 2008, which would strand and expose tens of thousands of remaining American trainers and advisers. Proposals to actually withdraw all U.S. forces on a fixed timetable are dismissed as "precipitous," when it seems much more precipitous to abandon thousands of Americans embedded in an unstable Iraqi military.

But the limitations of the critics' proposals pale in con-

---

[10] James Fallows, *Blind into Baghdad: America's War in Iraq* (Vintage, 2006), p. 182.

trast with the desperate expansionism of a besieged President Bush, who seems determined to carry this war forward into the term of his successor and possibly escalate a confrontation with Iran. Iraq has become a "march to folly," the phrase used by the late historian Barbara Tuchman to describe rulers who take a disastrous course, are offered reasonable alternatives, and yet insist on nonetheless continuing their reckless behavior.

There are genuine problems, of course, with any withdrawal, even from an unwinnable war. In this book, I hope to shift the discourse to the actual alternatives that lie ahead, by offering explanations of two important factors which receive little mainstream attention. First, *how could the U.S. government and armed forces be losing to, or at least not prevailing over, the Iraqi insurgency?* Rather than pointing toward mistaken prewar plans (not enough troops, no attention to reconstruction, etc.), it is more important to understand why the national, cultural, and religious resistance of Iraqis to the U.S. occupation may well be permanent and undefeatable. Such an assessment will be difficult for the superpower mentality to absorb, but could lead to the conclusion that ending the occupation is a necessity, not simply a choice.

Second, *while the new post-'60s antiwar movement is given little credit as a factor in turning public opinion against the war, it is a powerful force.* On eight occasions the movement has produced over 100,000 protesters in the streets, including three in which more than a half-million turned out to demonstrate. Public opinion has shifted against this conflict more rapidly than it did during the Vietnam War. At least 165 city councils and state legislatures have passed referendums against the war. Internet activism far surpasses the membership drives of antiwar groups in the '60s. The 2003–04 Howard Dean presidential campaign was in many ways similar to Eugene McCarthy's unsuccessful bid for the White House in 1967–68. And in November 2006, for the first time in U.S. history, American voters resolutely marched to the polls to reject an ongoing war.

Yet to many people, including activists, this war seems unstoppable and the opposition movement marginal or irrelevant. This is in part due to the media, but also to the Pentagon's strategy of lessening the direct impact of Iraq on the lives of most American citizens. There is no draft, we pay no direct taxes, the casualty rate of U.S. troops is one-fifteenth that of Vietnam. The perception of political impotence is also affected by anachronistic paradigms that contain romantic images of clashes in the streets of Chicago and the like. Bloggers against the war simply are not as dashing and photogenic as young men burning their draft cards in Central Park.

But this argument should be turned upside down: It is remarkable that the antiwar movement has become a catalyst of public opinion given all the resources expended on selling the Iraq War as cheap, easy, and non-intrusive in the lives of most Americans. It is a mistake to define the antiwar movement as narrowly confined to the streets, as political activism since the 1960s has opened up a space for working within a previously closed system. Bloggers and "netroots" have further developed this space, in a literal sense, through online activism.

It is necessary to write the antiwar movement into the history of this time.

This book also proposes a specific plan to end the war: by applying public pressure to the pillars of the war policy. All wars are dependent upon the availability of certain resources, which I label as *pillars*, and which are subject to individual, local, and movement pressures. The pillars which are needed to sustain this war, detailed in Chapter 4, include: [1] a stable ally in the form of an Iraqi government; [2] sufficient public support in America; [3] compliant American media outlets; [4] strong political support from the U.S. Congress; [5] an adequate supply of American troops and recruits; [6] ample budgetary resources over a decade-long period; [7] a moral reputation drawing respect at home and abroad; and [8] a network of international alliances, the so-called "coalition of the willing." Since the war began, we have seen all of these pillars gradually disintegrating. As they fall, the war will come to an end out of necessity. Those Machiavellians deeply concerned about damage to America's status will be forced to adopt a face-saving formula and leave Iraq.

Even assuming the administration expands the war to Iran (or Syria), this analysis would remain the same. A U.S. attack on Iran would be implausible, contradictory, and tragically ironic. The U.S. invaded and is occupying a country on Iran's long border, yet says that any Iranian interference in its neighbor's affairs could be a casus belli. Iran's alleged material involvement is at this point blamed for five percent of American deaths, according to a U.S. intelligence estimate.[11] The role of Saudi Arabia, an American ally, in providing support for the Sunni insurgents who attack American forces day in and day out goes unmentioned. Since the U.S. already pays for, trains, and props up Iranian-backed Shi'a militias in Iraq, the administration's new rhetoric sounds like scapegoating for a failed policy.

Presumably the rationale for an attack on Iran would be to degrade its infrastructure and suspected nuclear facilities, weakening the country's bid to become the main power in the

[11] David Blair, "Pentagon Blames Iran for 170 U.S. Deaths," *Daily Telegraph* (U.K.), February 12, 2007.

region. But such an escalation, launched primarily through bombing campaigns from aircraft carriers, would unite most Iranians and world opinion against the U.S., and leave American troops in Iraq exposed to a massive ground assault by Iranian forces from over the border. The pillars of the U.S. policy—most notably a lack of available American ground troops for the operation—would collapse entirely, tempting the White House to either disengage or deploy nuclear weapons.[12] Congress would require an authorization for any action against Iran. The public would favor diplomacy over preventive war. Talk of impeachment would increase and Republicans would face devastating losses in the 2008 elections. Any lasting solution would still require diplomacy and the withdrawal of American troops.

The roots of conflict with Iran are also buried in hidden memories, as the U.S. and U.K., driven by oil interests, deposed the country's nationalist prime minister to reinstate a repressive and compliant shah in 1953. That was a contributing factor to the 1979 Iranian Revolution and helps account for the country's continuing hostility to the United States. Some of the very "experts" who pushed the U.S. into war with Iraq in 2002–03 cannot understand today why Iran doesn't get over its "emotional baggage" from the U.S. overthrow of its leadership fifty years ago.[13] Superpowers may carry baggage them-

---

[12] According to Seymour Hersh, the White House considered the nuclear option against Iran's facilities at Natanz, but was opposed by the military leadership. See "Last Stand: The Military's Problem with the President's Iran Policy," *New Yorker*, July 10–17, 2006.

[13] See Kenneth M. Pollack, *The Persian Puzzle: The Conflict Between Iran and America* (Random House, 2005), p. 398. Pollack wrote *The Threatening Storm: The Case for Invading Iraq* (Random House) in late 2002, and served as a national security adviser on the Middle East. His later volume, *The Persian Puzzle*, is more tempered, but is saturated with elitist and Western-centric suppositions. He complains that the Iranians he has met continually harp on the theme of respect without ever explaining themselves. Pollack lists eight cases of "disrespectful" behavior he has heard, without emphasizing the core issue that

selves, making it impossible to admit legitimate Iranian and Middle Eastern grievances.

Even if war with Iran is avoided, many of the "best and brightest" who favored the Iraq War will scrub the history (and their resumes) to make it appear as only a slip-up or a case of not sending enough American troops to Iraq under a more competent administration. The idea that this war was in some sense *inevitable* given America's oil interests and political designs for the Middle East—especially with the intoxication of preeminence coming after the Cold War—is closer to the mark.

Whether crucial postwar "lessons" are heeded will help determine whether future wars become more or less likely. Wars, like social movements, begin and end with memories and monuments. There are war museums and monuments to unknown soldiers but no memorials for unknown peace activists. These can be built, and laws can be passed, however, by future generations that seek to prevent the same follies from being repeated. An important lesson from Iraq may be that responsibility for losing the war should rest with disciples of the superpower mentality, rather than with the antiwar movement, liberal Democrats, or, more broadly, the American people.

The essential question is whether working for peace is in America's best interest as a democratic republic. Just like the ghost of "Vietnam Syndrome," which the first Bush Administration tried to exorcise in Kuwait, a new "Iraq Syndrome" is beginning to appear. Americans will only be able to turn to our

---

the 1953 U.S.-instigated coup violated Iran's sovereignty and set in motion an enduring conflict between America and Iran. This is the "emotional baggage" that makes Iran "simply not ready for a meaningful relationship with the United States" (pp. 396–7). It may also be the rational, strategic consideration behind Iran's energy and security policies.

nation's other pressing priorities—and become safer and more respected across the globe—by heeding the call of the peace movement and ending the war in Iraq.

Tom Hayden
Los Angeles, CA
May 2007

CHAPTER 1

FROM VIETNAM SYNDROME TO IRAQ SYNDROME

There was a foreign policy consensus back then, and its disintegration during Vietnam is one of the great disasters of our history. You need an Establishment. Society needs it.

—Henry Kissinger[1]

We sensed it very early and very quickly. We saw the same destructive patterns reasserting themselves all over again as our leaders spoke of "bad guys" and "evil-doers," "imminent threats" and "mushroom clouds," attempting to frighten and intimidate the American people into supporting their agenda. The Bush Administration seems to have learned some very different lessons than we did from Vietnam. Where we learned of the deep immorality and obscenity of that war, they learned to be even more brutal, more violent and ruthless, i.e., "shock and awe."

—Ron Kovic[2]

Social movements rise, fall, and rise again in memory. The U.S. government, military, and media went to extraordinary lengths to purge what they called the Vietnam Syndrome from popular memory in the three decades following the war. When the first President Bush triumphed

---

[1] Walter Isaacson and Evan Thomas, *The Wise Men: Six Friends and the World They Made* (Simon & Schuster, 1997), pp. 736–7.
[2] Ron Kovic, *Born on the Fourth of July* (Akashic Books, 2005), p. 22. From Kovic's new introduction to the book, written in March 2005.

in the 1991 Gulf War, he declared, "By God, we've kicked the Vietnam Syndrome once and for all."[3]

The use of the word "syndrome" was borrowed from a mental health model, suggesting that something went deeply wrong with the American psyche during the war in Vietnam. The most significant antiwar movement in American history caught decision makers unaware. Rather than celebrating the healthy irreverence of millions of Americans who opposed the Vietnam conflict, the government and, to an extent, the media stigmatized the opposition as everything from isolationists to hippies to those unwilling to stand up to Communism.

The U.S. government never officially acknowledged defeat in Vietnam—Machiavellians cannot. Instead, efforts were launched to retroactively win the war in memory and myth.

First, in popular culture, there were films like the *Rambo* series which provided comforting fantasies rather than depicting the harsh realities of war. In *Rambo III*, John Rambo and the Afghan mujahideen fight together against the occupying Soviet Army in an unintentionally iconic portrayal of U.S. Cold War policy. (Ironically, the actor and my friend Sylvester Stallone avoided service in the Vietnam War.)

Second, tales were concocted of antiwar hippies "spitting" on returning soldiers. So powerful was this myth that, for a time, I myself thought it must be true, even though I'd never seen evidence of an actual example. In 1998, the Vietnam veteran and sociologist Jerry Lembcke, after exhaustive research, could not find any references to these instances of spitting in the media of the late '60s and early '70s.[4] It was a myth that discredited antiwar activists effectively.

[3] Cited in George C. Herring, "America and Vietnam: The Unending War," *Foreign Affairs*, Winter 1991/1992.
[4] See Jerry Lembcke, *The Spitting Image: Myth, Memory, and the Legacy of Vietnam* (New York University Press, 1998). A 1995 study by Richard Flacks, Har-

Third, claims were made that the Vietnam War was "necessary" to hold the line against Communism until it bled to death by overextension. In these revisionist histories, Ho Chi Minh was portrayed as a Moscow-serving Stalinist, not a genuinely popular national independence leader.[5] The 1968 Tet Offensive was described as a military failure for the Vietcong and a propaganda victory for Hanoi, despite what actually transpired.

These efforts at justifying the Vietnam War—indeed, re-fighting it on the field of memory—came down to eliminating the Vietnam Syndrome, which can be reduced to these antiwar propositions that had settled deeply into America's consciousness:

- "*No more Vietnams*," meaning no future land wars leading to significant American casualties;
- "*America cannot be the policeman of the world*," defined as avoiding interventions in foreign conflicts where American security was not at stake;
- "*End the imperial presidency*," referring to the growth

vey Molotch, and Thomas D. Beamish of 495 stories mentioning veterans and antiwar protesters found that only six percent over six years could be construed as antagonistic to Vietnam soldiers or veterans, and no cases of spitting were reported ("Who Supports the Troops? Vietnam, the Gulf War, and Collective Memory," *Social Problems*, August 1995). Lembcke also noted a survey of national opinion polls between 1968 and 1973 showing no evidence that the public even thought that acts of hostility toward Vietnam veterans were occurring. Finally, a 1971 Harris poll of returning veterans found that ninety-four percent felt a friendly reception from Americans their own age, as opposed to three percent who believed their reception was "not at all friendly" (Lembcke, p. 75). Incredibly, the only incidents of spitting that were reported anywhere were of *pro-war* individuals, sometimes older veterans, who apparently spit on returning Vietnam veterans for losing.

[5] See Michael Lind, *Vietnam, The Necessary War: A Reinterpretation of America's Most Disastrous Military Conflict* (Free Press, 1999). He says the U.S. fought the war out of geopolitical necessity, but gave up due to domestic pressures. There are many factual errors—among them, his claim that I received a White House freedom award from President Jimmy Carter (p. 208).

of the national security state beyond the oversight of Congress, the media, and the American public;
• *"Heal the wounds of war,"* calling for better treatment of Vietnam veterans, amnesty for Americans who had moved to Canada to avoid the compulsory draft, and reconciliation rather than recrimination both within the U.S. and between Americans and the Vietnamese.

This consensus threatened the Cold Warriors who led the nation into Vietnam. From their viewpoint, it signified retreat from global military responsibilities, success of an "excess of democracy"[6] over traditional authority structures, and increased legitimacy for protest movements. The result was seen as an unwillingness by Americans to shed their children's blood and part with taxes necessary for sustaining a global war-making capacity.

But the Vietnam Syndrome, far from being a weakness, was a corrective sense of suspicion toward American institutions, derived from the experience of the '60s generation—one sharply different from that of U.S. citizens during World War II and the Korean War.

Like many American families, mine was divided and broken over the Vietnam War. My father, a World War II marine, stopped speaking to me, or even acknowledging that I was his son, for a period of sixteen years. His generation believed that all of America's problems were caused by maligned foreign powers—Japan, Germany, and ultimately the Soviet Union. In his view, war was a necessary response to these external

---

[6] "Excess of democracy" was the terminology of Samuel Huntington, in a presentation to the secretive Trilateral Commission and other writings in the '70s. Also adopting a medical model, Huntington wrote of a "democratic distemper." See Michel J. Crozier, Samuel P. Huntingon, and Joji Watanuki, *The Crisis of Democracy: Report on the Governability of Democracies to the Trilateral Commission* (New York University Press, 1975).

threats. For my generation, the problems were on the home front, in our battles against racial segregation, poverty, and the treatment of students as powerless dependents who could be drafted for war but could not vote. These problems were not due to the Soviet Union or international Communism, but rather to the stratification of American society itself. When the Vietnam War began, it seemed to many of us a wasteful diversion from the crises in our own backyard. For example, I was a community organizer in the Newark ghetto, where the issues of housing, police brutality, garbage collection, and simmering racial violence seemed far more urgent than dispatching troops to bring the Great Society to the Mekong Delta.

More significant was my generation's dawning perception that the government lied on matters of life and death, as when Johnson campaigned in 1964 on a platform of avoiding a ground war in Southeast Asia. His post-election betrayal was bitterly felt—the opposite experience of my marine father's trust in his commander-in-chief—and it would cause permanent gaps in understanding along generational lines.

Antiwar sentiment reflected the wider questioning of authority which exploded during the '60s. Millions of Americans, especially people of color and students, drew conclusions that went beyond the Vietnam War to question "the system" itself. The growing radicalism was perceived as a threat to the stability of American institutions by the Machiavellian class. For example:

• By the late 1960s—in the face of police repression, shootings, and beatings—civil disobedience, street fighting, and takeovers of administration buildings became common in the student, antiwar, and draft resistance movements; the years 1968–70 included the largest student strikes and campus shutdowns in history. There were notable confrontations at the Pentagon (October 1967), at the Democratic Convention in Chicago (August 1968), during the Chicano Moratorium march in east Los Angeles (August 1970), and on May Day (1971). There was also the rise of the Weather Underground (1969–1970).

• There were scores of riots and insurrections in black communities during the height of the war, from 1965 to 1968, causing the blue-ribbon Kerner Commission to warn in 1968 that America was evolving into two societies, separate and unequal.

• This same conflict was mirrored in the American armed forces, where at least 600 soldiers attempted to kill their commanding officers in so-called "fraggings," and nearly a half-million soldiers were dishonorably discharged.[7]

• The spirit of defiance was embodied by Vietnam Veterans Against the War, an organization founded in 1967 that engaged in petitioning, marches, and acts of civil disobedience, including throwing their medals and Purple Hearts on the steps of the Capitol in April 1971.

This polarization, which tore apart families and in many ways the nation itself, was viewed by the elites as a serious *cost* of the Vietnam War. Was the war worth the evident alienation of future generations, the growing racial violence in Ameri-

[7] Chris Hedges, *What Every Person Should Know About War* (Free Press, 2003), p. 85.

can cities, or the mutinies in the U.S. armed forces? Would the "excess of democracy" perceived by Huntington produce "problems for the governability of democracy" in the 1970s?

While many protesters felt no one was listening, the establishment itself was threatened to its bones. When demonstrators descended on the Pentagon in October 1967, Lady Bird Johnson wrote in her diary that "there is a ripple of grim excitement in the air, almost a feeling of being under siege."[8] The next day, CIA director Richard Helms stood with Pentagon officials, protected by army snipers, and reflected, "Nobody liked the look of that at all. And I certainly least of all. I'd had experiences with mobs all over the world and I didn't like the look or sound of this one bit."[9] In fact, the lasting image from the Pentagon incident was of peaceful protesters placing flowers in the bayoneted barrels of soldiers' guns—yet it seemed like the siege of Leningrad to officials grown too comfortable with their isolation from the American public.

There was a cultural lag time between positions which seemed "radical" at first but steadily became acceptable in mainstream discourse, nowhere more evident than in public attitudes toward the Vietnam War. By the middle of 1967, a Gallup poll showed that for the first time a majority of Americans disapproved of Johnson's handling of the war.[10] Senator Eugene McCarthy announced his peace candidacy in November of that year, declaring that he wanted to create a channel within the system to harness the energy of young radicals. Discounted by the establishment, the young McCarthy volunteers stunned Johnson in the snows of New Hampshire with a close second-place finish, amassing forty-two percent of the

[8] Cited in Jonathan Neale, *A People's History of the Vietnam War* (New Press, 2003), p. 132.
[9] Neale, p. 133.
[10] Gallup poll, July 30, 1967.

primary vote and holding the president to just under fifty percent. McCarthy's success impelled Senator Robert Kennedy into the presidential race the following week.

Facing these threats, President Johnson summoned a group of senior advisers from diplomatic, corporate, and military backgrounds. These characters from the pages of C. Wright Mills's 1956 book *The Power Elite* were dubbed the "Wise Men" by Johnson. During two days of private meetings in the White House, the president was counseled that the war was unwinnable, counterproductive, and threatened the domestic order. The shocking result was Johnson's announcement that he would not seek a second term as president. These developments will be further analyzed in the chapters ahead.

Catastrophe rained down in 1968, including the murders of Martin Luther King Jr. and Robert Kennedy, and culminating in the street confrontations at the August Democratic National Convention in Chicago. I am convinced that Robert Kennedy could have been elected president, ended the war, and formed a progressive alliance with the movements represented by Dr. King. Such possibilities have been largely excised from the usual narratives of the 1960s. What happened in Chicago was an orchestrated effort by the pro-Nixon FBI director, J. Edgar Hoover, to repeat the experience of 1950s McCarthyism by demonizing and jailing the "Chicago Eight" and other antiwar radicals. While he failed to suppress dissent, Hoover certainly contributed to the climate of "law and order" that helped elect Nixon and usher in the next generation of conservatives. On Vietnam, Nixon was able to manipulate and delay the peace talks proposed by Johnson, while implying that he had a "secret plan for peace," thus denying the Democrats the last-minute triumph they needed to prevail in the election.[11] Faced with murder, repression, and dirty tricks, the New Left was denied its opportunity to prevail as part of a new political majority.

The war went on. The period of 1969–72 was one of cascading blood from Vietnamese, Cambodian, and Laotian bodies, as the U.S. combined troop withdrawals with unprecedented bombings of Indochina, exceeding the cumulative tonnage of bombs the U.S. had dropped in Europe during World War II.[12] The numbers of American soldiers killed would roughly double during Nixon's first term, while deaths among the Indochinese people would reach an estimated two million, with another four million wounded or turned into refugees. Peace talks stalled while the struggle for victory continued on the battlefield.

Yet peace sentiment continued to spread across the U.S. No longer in power and responsible for maintaining the war, many Democrats now tilted toward the antiwar opposition. A broader and more moderate peace coalition, called the Moratorium to End the War in Vietnam, organized demonstrations that convened an estimated one million people in Washington, D.C. and the San Francisco Bay Area in 1969. A radical coalition known as the Mayday Tribe tried to "stop the government" in 1971, shutting down the streets of Washington until mass detention orders resulted in an unprecedented 13,000 people being held without charges in RFK Stadium.[13]

Even after the withdrawal of U.S. troops, the peace

---

[11] Nixon attempted to make inroads with the center. Shortly after the 1968 convention, I was invited to meet the television correspondent Mike Wallace, who tried to persuade me to support this "new Nixon." Later, Nixon speechwriter William Safire showed me a campaign speech on participatory democracy, saying, "This one was written for you." The apparent idea was to pull discontented radicals or liberals away from Humphrey, or encourage them not to vote. In any event, Nixon won by less than one percent.

[12] Daniel Ellsberg, *Secrets: A Memoir of Vietnam and the Pentagon Papers* (Penguin, 2003), p. 420.

[13] Ellsberg, p. 381.

movement continued to operate. In 1972 and 1973, the Indochina Peace Campaign organized rallies, educational presentations, and grassroots coalitions to lobby for an end to congressional funding of the war.[14] Nixon became more aggressive as he recognized a deepening crisis. Facing defeat, he considered deploying nuclear weapons, but chose everything short of that option, as reflected in this exchange with Secretary of State Henry Kissinger:

> N: *And I still think we ought to take the dikes out now. Will that drown people?*
> K: *About two hundred thousand people.*
> N: *No, no, no . . . I'd rather use the nuclear bomb. Have you got that, Henry?*
> K: *That, I think, would be just too much.*
> N: *The nuclear bomb, does that bother you? . . . I just want you to think big, Henry, for chrissakes.*[15]

One week later, Nixon was raving again:

> *I want that place bombed to smithereens. If we draw the sword, we're gonna bomb those bastards all over the place . . . We're going to cream them . . . For once we've got to use the maximum power of this country . . . against this shit-ass little country, to win the war.*[16]

---

[14] This was a group of New Left, pacifist, clergy, and local organizations that generated pressure on Congress from pivotal states including California, New York, New Jersey, Massachusetts, Pennsylvania, Ohio, Michigan, and Illinois. The "star" was my then-wife Jane Fonda. With former POWs and artists, we barnstormed through a hundred cities, building coalitions coordinated through a Washington office. The so-called "congressional strategy" was meant to supplement and focus the energy of demonstrations in the streets. When the plan succeeded, the organization dissolved.

[15] Ellsberg, p. 418.

[16] Ellsberg, p. 419.

And on civilian casualties, Nixon said to Kissinger:

The only place where you and I disagree . . . is with regard to bombing. You're so goddamned concerned about the civilians and I don't give a damn. I don't care. [17]

I include these taped quotations as an example of how presidents, then and perhaps now, approach their alternatives when hanging on the brink of failure.

After promising "peace with honor" and having Kissinger declare "peace is at hand" during the 1972 presidential campaign, the U.S. dropped 20,000 tons of bombs on Hanoi during an eleven-day period over Christmas, then signed a peace agreement on January 27, leading to the final withdrawal of U.S. troops and release of American prisoners.[18] Thus, Nixon could claim to be negotiating from a position of strength, even though the U.S. lost more B-52s over Hanoi than during the entirety of the previous war. The Paris agreement provided a two-year "decent interval,"[19] in Kissinger's discreet language, between the American pullout and the final battle for South Vietnam in 1975, which concluded with a disorderly U.S. retreat from its own embassy and a takeover by Vietcong and North Vietnamese forces.

Attempting to continue the war despite huge public

[17] "Nixon Had Notion to Use Nuclear Bomb in Vietnam," *USA Today*, February 28, 2002.
[18] Ellsberg, p. 418.
[19] One page of Kissinger's briefing book for his 1971 discussions in China contained a written promise, in his own handwriting: "We need a decent interval. You have our assurance." See Jeffrey Kimball, "The Case of the 'Decent Interval': Do We Now Have a Smoking Gun?" *Society for Historians of American Foreign Relations Newsletter*, September 2001. Kimball cites the briefing as *POLO II (Part I), Box 850, NSC. For the President's Files (Winston Lord)—China Trip/Vietnam, NPM.* Another Kissinger document speaks of a *"healthy interval for South Vietnam's fate to unfold."* See Jeffrey Kimball, *The Vietnam War Files: Uncovering the Secret History of Nixon-Era Strategy* (University Press of Kansas, 2003).

opposition, President Nixon engaged in First Amendment violations, most famously the Watergate scandal. Eventually, congressional impeachment hearings were launched, and Nixon was forced to resign the presidency on August 9, 1974. It was not until the Watergate crisis that Congress voted to cut off funds for combat and bombing operations in Vietnam through the Foreign Assistance Act of 1974, which President Gerald Ford signed into law on December 30. The Saigon regime collapsed on April 30, 1975.

The Nixon era came to an end at the same time as long gas lines began to appear in Washington, while the rise of the Organization of Petroleum Exporting Countries (OPEC)—a cartel of nationalist, oil-producing regimes—was made possible in part by the decline of the U.S. as a military hegemon. As a result, a movement for conservation and renewable energy resources was on the rise, as were the organizing efforts of Ralph Nader and the political fortunes of California governor Jerry Brown. It was a bright moment for social change. I organized a grassroots economic and environmental movement in California and became the state's official solar energy advocate. Brown's campaign was absorbed by Jimmy Carter, elected president in 1976.

The peace movement, beginning at the margins ten years before, had broadened its ranks and finally achieved a spectacular victory. The elites had failed to secure a face-saving cover for their defeat. The widely accepted lessons of the war served as normative barriers against further U.S. interventions for several years:

- In 1976, Congress voted to end funding for CIA operations in Angola;
- President Jimmy Carter ordered an amnesty for

the estimated 50,000 American war deserters in Canada;

• In response to the Pinochet dictatorship, President Carter and Congress banned military sales and assistance to Chile in 1976;

• Carter established human rights standards as new principles of U.S. foreign policy;

• In Central America, revolution was on the march. The Boland Amendment of 1982–84 limited intelligence-agency funding for the Contras in Nicaragua and banned U.S. forces from operating in that country.

The ruling elite was alarmed at these developments. Huntington's warnings about the "excess of democracy" resonated in the corridors of power. Lewis Powell, a future Supreme Court justice, penned an influential August 1971 confidential memo for the U.S. Chamber of Commerce, titled "Attack of American Free Enterprise System."[20] Powell's proposal, which he described as "not one for the fainthearted," called for a corporate united front to achieve the political power necessary for protecting the free enterprise system in the next generation. Powell advocated funding "scholars who do believe in the system," the critical evaluation of textbooks, changing the balance of faculties, monitoring television for anticorporate bias, spending ten percent of corporate advertising dollars on generic pro-business ads, funding legal advocacy before the court, and direct political action to neutralize the "anti-business views now being expressed by several leading candidates for President of the United States."

In response to the radical shift flowing from the 1960s— almost half of American students favored socialization of ba-

---

[20] Powell's memo, dated August 23, 1971, was leaked to syndicated columnist Jack Anderson.

sic U.S. industries, Powell claimed—corporate America began funding a long-term counterattack.

THE NEOCONSERVATIVES' WAR AGAINST IRAQ AND THE '60S

This is not ancient history: Vietnam and Watergate served as formative experiences for those who advocated war against Iraq only one generation later. They were fighting to rid America of the Vietnam Syndrome, and any trace elements of 1960s consciousness.

Several strands of conservative counterrevolution resulted in the election of Ronald Reagan. First, reactionary Southerners were attracted by Reagan's symbolic choice of launching his 1980 presidential campaign in Neshoba County, Mississippi, the racist stronghold where three civil rights workers were kidnapped and murdered in the summer of 1964. Second, the fast-growing Christian evangelical movement cultivated by Reagan in 1980 threw themselves into politics in a "culture war" against 1960s radicalism. Third, traditional conservatives clustered around publications like the *National Review*, which had supported segregation as recently as the early '60s and had a rigid agenda that was strongly pro-business, anti-government, and anti-Communist. After recovering from the stinging defeat of Barry Goldwater in 1964, they attempted to build a conservative majority and take over the Republican Party from within.

But it was a loose faction of so-called *neoconservatives* who fashioned the most aggressive platform against the New Left and the 1960s zeitgeist; they would attain positions of power during the 1980s and ultimately lobby successfully for the invasion of Iraq. As told by neoconservative Francis Fukuyama:

*American politics had shifted dramatically by the late
1960s, as a result of the civil rights movement and the
Vietnam War, the old Communist and fellow-traveling left
of left of the 1930s had been replaced, at least temporarily,
by the New Left of Tom Hayden and the Students for a
Democratic Society . . .*

   *The first formative battle that shaped neoconserva-
tism was the fight with the Stalinists of the '30s and '40s;
the second was the one with the New Left and the counterculture it spawned in the 1960s. The second battle had
both foreign and domestic policy dimensions.*[21]

Those who became known as neoconservatives had been
fierce adversaries of the early SDS. The Cold War debates of
four decades ago foreshadowed those of today. The SDS Port
Huron Statement (1962) broke from Cold War thinking by
claiming that "an unreasoning anti-Communism has become
a major social problem for those who want to construct a more
democratic America."[22] We noted the hypocrisy of our government supporting a dictator like Ngo Dinh Diem in South
Vietnam while waging war against Fidel Castro's Cuba. Though
critical of the Soviet Union, we refused to believe that Moscow
was inherently driven to take over Europe and the rest of the

[21] Francis Fukuyama, *America at the Crossroads: Democracy, Power, and the Neoconservative Legacy* (Yale University Press, 2006), pp. 17–18. It is reported that I
sent the SDS founding document, the Port Huron Statement, to neoconservative leader Norman Podhoretz in 1961, and that it was rejected as "intellectually shallow." If so, I have no recollection of the correspondence, though I did
send an article about the New Left, which Podhoretz did reject, and which I
still possess, unpublished. On this confused matter, see Murray Friedman, *The
Neoconservative Revolution: Jewish Intellectuals and the Shaping of Public Policy*
(Cambridge University Press, 2005), p. 123.
[22] Tom Hayden, *The Port Huron Statement: The Visionary Call of the 1960s Revolution* (Thunder's Mouth, 2005), p. 103. See also, Tom Hayden, *Rebel: A Personal History of the 1960s* (Red Hen Press, 2003), p. 79–83.

world. Instead, we favored peaceful coexistence, a reversal of the arms race, and greater investment in economic development at home and abroad. These views were inexcusably "soft on Communism," according to leaders of our parent organization, the League for Industrial Democracy, like Tom Kahn and Rachelle Horowitz, who suspended SDS staff (Al Haber and myself) and locked us out of our New York offices. SDS eventually restored itself, but the divisions only deepened in the following decade. Kahn, Horowitz, and their allies strongly supported the Vietnam War based on their anti-Communist ideology. Kahn became chief speechwriter for the AFL-CIO's George Meany, an ardent anti-Communist hawk; Horowitz became a top leader of the American Federation of Teachers and married Tom Donahue, secretary-treasurer of the AFL-CIO. From such anti-Communist and social democratic roots grew sharp divisions in the Democratic Party and eventually the realignment that led to neoconservatism.

Various neoconservative factions are rooted in a common hostility toward the radicalism of the 1960s and a commitment to suppress the Vietnam Syndrome. Many, though far from all, are dedicated Jewish supporters of Israel—with a special animus against Arab nationalists and liberal sympathizers with the Palestinian people—and, paradoxically, have developed an especially strong solidarity with Christian evangelicals whose commitment to Israel is based on their interpretation of Armageddon and the Second Coming.

FBI Director J. Edgar Hoover launched public campaigns and counterintelligence programs against the New Left, beginning in 1960 with "Communist Target—Youth" and secret directives to "neutralize" black and antiwar activists in 1968.[23]

[23] Seth Rosenfeld, "Reagan, Hoover and the UC Red Scare," *San Francisco Chronicle*, June 9, 2002.

George W. Bush was a high school cheerleader who avoided the draft, the antiwar movement, and any association with counterculture. "I got into politics initially because I wanted to help change a culture," he told conservative columnist David Brooks in 2006.[24]

Vice President *Dick Cheney* and his wife *Lynne*, University of Wisconsin graduate students in 1967, were stepping over the bodies of fellow students blockading buildings in protest of the Vietnam War.[25] In 1968, Cheney worked on legislation for a Republican congressman to cut off federal funding to universities where protests were occurring.[26] Lynne Cheney became a ferocious critic of 1960s curriculum reforms during her tenure at the National Endowment for the Humanities.

Karl Rove leaped into high school classroom discussions "denouncing Tom Hayden and the Weathermen and Students for a Democratic Society," according to a biography.[27] He became executive director of the College Republicans during the Watergate period, allied himself with Young Americans for Freedom, and specialized in dirty tricks, which he called "pranks."[28]

Ronald Reagan came to power attacking the "filthy speech movement" (or the Free Speech Movement of 1964–65) at the University of California, Berkeley. He collaborated with the FBI to identify radical professors and unseat the UC president, Clark Kerr.[29]

Edwin Meese, later U.S. Attorney General and conserva-

[24] David Brooks, "Ends Without Means," *New York Times*, September 14, 2006.
[25] David Maraniss, *They Marched Into Sunlight: War and Peace, Vietnam and America, October 1967* (Simon & Schuster, 2003), pp. 514–6.
[26] Dan Briody, *The Halliburton Agenda: The Politics of Oil and Money* (Wiley, 2004), p. 193.
[27] James Moore and Wayne Slater, *Bush's Brain: How Karl Rove Made George W. Bush Presidential* (Wiley, 2003), p. 124.
[28] Moore and Slater, pp. 130–1.
[29] Seth Rosenfeld, "Ex-UC Chief Calls FBI Actions Despicable," *San Francisco Chronicle*, June 10, 2002.

tive leader, was Reagan's chief of staff and the former Alameda County prosecutor of campus radicals.

James Q. Wilson chaired the Harvard faculty committee which disciplined student protesters in the late 1960s.[30]

Samuel P. Huntington, another Harvard professor who later wrote *The Clash of Civilizations*, authored the doctrine of "forced urbanization" for South Vietnamese peasants in 1969, as well as the presentation previously mentioned decrying the 1960s "excess of democracy" to the elite Trilateral Commission.

William Bennett became the leading critic of multiculturalism and "political correctness" as head of the National Endowment for the Humanities under Reagan.

William Kristol, son of the neoconservative founders Irving Kristol and Gertrude Himmelfarb, was William Bennett's chief of staff. The elder Kristol had traveled from the Young People's Socialist League in the 1930s to become editor of *Encounter*, a magazine indirectly funded by the CIA, and then a leading defender of Senator Joseph McCarthy in the 1950s.[31] As a Harvard student during the 1960s, his son William began a magazine that became the *American Spectator*, lashing out against campus liberals and radicals, and extolling Nixon's 1972 bombing of North Vietnam as "one of the great moments in American history."[32] William would rise to become chief aide to Vice President Dan Quayle, who campaigned against Candice Bergen for violating "family values" by playing a single mother on the television program *Murphy Brown*.

William Kristol came under the spell of *Leo Strauss* at the University of Chicago. Strauss was a philosopher of Machiavelli who believed in an elitist doctrine of necessary deception.

---

[30] Nina J. Easton, *Gang of Five: Leaders at the Center of the Conservative Crusade* (Simon & Schuster, 2000), p. 25.
[31] Easton, p. 33.
[32] Easton, p. 27.

These "Straussians" overlapped with the disciples of another Chicago theorist, *Albert Wohlstetter*, whose strategic writings foreshadowed the Bush doctrine of preventive war. Wohlstetter too was driven by a fear that the legacy of the 1960s would restrict future U.S. military interventions, including action to secure the oil of the Middle East.[33]

Among Wohlstetter's leading protégés was *Paul Wolfowitz*, the principle architect of the 2003 invasion of Iraq.

Elliott Abrams is of particular significance, both because of his longevity and his continuing importance to President George W. Bush on Middle East policy for the National Security Council. He married into one of the most prominent neoconservative first-families, that of Norman Podhoretz and Midge Decter, and was a frequent contributor to Podhoretz's *Commentary* magazine. During the Reagan years, Abrams was charged with deceiving Congress in the Iran-Contra affair, only to later receive a presidential pardon from George H.W. Bush in 1992. He survived to return to the White House in 2005 as George W. Bush's point man on Israel and the Middle East; *Newsweek* called him "The Last Man Standing" among neoconservatives in 2006.[34]

There are many more neoconservatives, including *Richard Perle* and *John Bolton* (of the Project for the New American Century), *Gary Schmitt*, *Alan Keyes*, *Douglas Feith* (former DOD under-secretary for policy), *Stephen Cambone* (DOD under-secretary for intelligence), and *Abram Shulsky* (from the DOD Office of Special Plans), who deserve placement in a full sociogram.[35]

---

[33] Andrew J. Bacevich, *The New American Militarism: How Americans Are Seduced by War* (Oxford University Press, 2005), p. 164.
[34] Michael Hirsh and Dan Ephron, "The Last Man Standing," *Newsweek*, December 4, 2006.
[35] See, for example, Earl Shorris, "Ignoble Liars: Leo Strauss, George Bush, and the Philosophy of Mass Deception," *Harper's*, June 2004.

These neoconservatives have become known for leading America into the Iraq War, but the depth and staying power of their underlying resentment toward 1960s leftist movements is often forgotten. For the neoconservatives, all of Bill Clinton's shortcomings were attributed to 1960s "permissiveness," and their hatred of John Kerry was rooted in his 1960s involvement with Vietnam Veterans Against the War. Even in 2007, *Dinesh D'Souza* was blaming 9/11 and the Iraq War on the antiwar counterculture of the '60s for having alienated Muslims through our "decadence" that undermined "the traditional patriarchal family." His solution: Defeat liberalism. "Unlike [Joseph] McCarthy, who never disclosed the identities of the Communists and Soviet sympathizers in high places, I intend to name the enemy at home," he writes.[36]

By the 1990s, it appeared that the neoconservatives had triumphed over all foreign and domestic enemies. It was "the end of history," according to Fukuyama. From their circles, backed by well-funded conservative think tanks, came the drumbeat of policy papers calling for a New American Century, a play on the conservative call for an "American Century" at the dawn of the Cold War. In 1996, the same forces were advocating benevolent hegemony in the pages of Kristol's new magazine, the *Weekly Standard*, funded by Rupert Murdoch. In 1998, they lobbied President Clinton to overthrow Saddam Hussein,[37] a proposal which was also made to Israel's then–Prime Minister Benjamin Netanyahu. They predicted a short war, followed by a welcoming with flowers.

---

[36] Dinesh D'Souza, *The Enemy at Home: The Cultural Left and Its Responsibility for 9/11* (Doubleday, 2007), pp. 255, 289.
[37] Signers of the letter to Clinton included Elliott Abrams, William Bennett, John Bolton, Francis Fukuyama, Robert Kagan, Zalmay Khalilzad (who later became ambassador to Baghdad), William Kristol, Donald Rumsfeld, Paul Wolfowitz, and James Woolsey. "Letter to President Clinton on Iraq," Project for the New American Century, January 26, 1998.

Overall, it appeared that the syndromes of the 1960s had indeed been pacified. The draft was gone. Eighteen-year-olds could vote, and even read Emma Goldman in the classroom instead of at the barricades. The Pentagon was intent on low-visibility warfare with minimal casualties and "supplemental" budget costs (that is, passed on to future generations). Information-based strategies were designed to keep the media at bay. With the 1991 Gulf War and Balkan conflicts throughout the 1990s, it seemed that the promise of war on the cheap (at least for Americans) had come true. Full-spectrum military dominance could be integrated with the "new world order" of trade and commerce foreseen by the first President Bush, and by the bipartisan consensus favoring the World Trade Organization (WTO). By 1999, just when protesters were about to derail the Seattle meeting of the WTO, Thomas Friedman wrote that the new system of globalization would need a military "enforcer"—a "new burden" that would fall to the United States.[38]

Then came the tragedy of September 11, 2001, which seemed to confirm the neoconservative ideology of a "clash of civilizations" that necessitated a "war on terror," a framework recalling the fifty years of Cold War that had come before. Even moderate voices were cast aside in the new consensus that war, retaliatory but also preventive, was imperative. Afghanistan was first; Iraq would follow.

Yet the Vietnam Syndrome lurked just beneath the surface of this apparent unanimity. Americans certainly favored military retaliation against whomever had attacked our country. But there was no such support for quagmires and all their corollaries. A survey showed that sixty-three percent of Americans still quietly believed that the Vietnam War had

[38] Thomas Friedman, "Manifesto for the Free World," *New York Times Magazine*, March 28, 1999.

been "fundamentally wrong."[39] Sixties radicalism, even in its seemingly sold-out, middle-aged dormancy, had become the common sense of the nation. While advocates of a "Goliath-like" approach to foreign policy such as Michael Mandelbaum believed that September 11 "seemed, at first, to provide a replacement for the Cold War," many Americans diverged from this perspective.[40]

Once again the obstacle was the 1960s generation, with its steadfast commitment to entitlement programs like health care and social security. As this demograpic had gained positions of power, Mandelbaum worried that "democracy [would] favor butter over guns," fearing that the Vietnam Syndrome would reappear and reject military interventions in favor of domestic social needs.[41] He wrote: "It will become increasingly difficult for the foreign policy elite to persuade the wider public to support the kinds of policies that, collectively, make up *the American role as the world's government.* Foreign policy will be relegated to the back burner"[42] [italics added for emphasis].

Mandelbaum was concerned that focusing on a domestic agenda would challenge America's attempts at empire—the very challenge that arose in the early 1960s. Shortly after the Vietnam War came the rise of OPEC and a flattening of middle-class incomes for the next thirty-five years. Families were working longer hours without seeing comparable pay increases. Working- and middle-class families found minimum wage, job tenure, comany pensions, and health insurance all in decline. The erosion of these social services was rationalized by an increase in untouchable expenditures on war

[39] Cited in Neale, p. 220.
[40] Michael Mandelbaum, *The Case for Goliath: How America Acts as the World's Government in the 21st Century* (PublicAffairs, 2005), p. 178.
[41] Mandelbaum, p. 185.
[42] Mandelbaum, pp. 185–6.

and national security. The case for Mandelbaum's Goliath was an easy sell to many Americans—until the catastrophe in Iraq.

By 2006, history had far from "ended." The neoconservatives were in retreat, or regrouping from the Baghdad debacle. Blood was on their hands, and scandals were surfacing. Wolfowitz, like Robert McNamara before him, had changed identity the previous year to become president of the World Bank, only to face calls for his resignation in April 2007 after providing promotions and pay raises to his girlfriend in a classic case of institutional nepotism.[43] Meanwhile, Perle and others were issuing their regrets to the readers of *Vanity Fair*. Bolton couldn't get the Senate to make him permanent UN ambassador. Ken Adelman, who had predicted the invasion would be a cakewalk, now wrote a virtual epitaph for the neoconservative movement, saying that "the idea of using our power for moral good in the world" had been discredited and "is not going to sell."[44] On the other hand, Fukuyama, in a powerful criticism of his neoconservative comrades, tried to save the doctrine itself from what he called its failures of implementation.

The worst news of all for pro-war hawks appeared in the November/December 2005 issue of *Foreign Affairs*, the journal of foreign policy elites. The article, by John Mueller of Ohio State University, announced the coming of the Iraq Syndrome.[45] Surveying public opinion polls, Mueller concluded that the previous Vietnam Syndrome was far from vanquished; like an ineradicable virus, it was mutating into a new form, the Iraq Syndrome. The "casualties" of this syn-

[43] Richard Adams, "World Bank 'In Crisis' Over Wolfowitz," *Guardian* (U.K.), April 16, 2007.
[44] David Rose, "Neo Culpa," *Vanity Fair*, November 3, 2006.
[45] John Mueller, "The Iraq Syndrome," *Foreign Affairs*, November/December 2005.

drome, he said, might well be the Bush doctrines of unilateralism, preventive war, and even the idea of America as
the "indispensable nation." Further, he noted growing public
skepticism toward such "key notions" as "having by far the
largest defense budget in the world is necessary and broadly
beneficial."

Nevertheless, when President Bush sought support for a
military "surge" in Iraq and increased pressure against Iran in
early 2007, he turned again to the diehard neoconservatives
who had never left their battle stations—Frederick Kagan and
the ubiquitous William Kristol—to lobby for an alternative to
the *Iraq Study Group Report*, which had been led by a bipartisan team cochaired by James Baker and Lee Hamilton. Backing the neoconservative thesis was James Q. Wilson, who
blamed the "liberal media" for failing to report positive news
from Iraq: "We lost in Vietnam and are in danger of losing in
Iraq and Lebanon in the newspapers, magazines, and television
programs we enjoy."[46]

President Bush was *expanding* the neoconservative agenda
despite its resounding defeat in the November 2006 election.
His strategy was almost entirely faith-based. The purpose of
American escalations in Vietnam, like this one in Baghdad,
had not been about winning (though that remained a faith-
based hope) but about *not losing*, and passing the venture
along from president to president. George H.W. Bush started
a war with Iraq over Kuwait, passed it along to Bill Clinton,
who signed the Iraq Liberation Act of 1998 to finance regime
change and then passed it along to George W. Bush and Dick
Cheney, who, after September 11 and the invasion of Afghanistan, launched the war in 2003 that they seemed to want all
along.

[46] James Q. Wilson, "The Press at War," *City Journal*, Autumn 2006.

By 2007, although virtually no Democratic voters and only twenty percent of Republicans supported sending more American soldiers to Baghdad, Bush and the neoconservatives were determined to surge.

Perhaps it was a perfect setup from the Bush Administration's standpoint. If the surge succeeded in its goal of preventing their mission in Iraq from failing, the war baton could be passed along to the eager John McCain (or Rudy Giuliani, who led early polls among Republican voters), or else dropped into the lap of the next Democratic president. If the escalation was rejected or thwarted, the neoconservatives could script a powerful postwar narrative claiming that Iraq was "lost" because of spineless '60s liberals—just as China, Korea, and Vietnam had been "lost" due to the similar domestic "enemies" over the previous fifty years.[47]

It is too early to know the verdict of historians, but the debacle can be traced to two blind spots in what the eminent therapist and Harvard scholar Robert Jay Lifton has called the "Superpower Syndrome"[48] in direct critique of the neoconservative diagnosis:

• The end of the Cold War never meant the end of nationalism, cultural pride, or revolution. As noted in Chapter 2, a top U.S. general said of the Iraqi nationalist and Islamic resistance, "We did not see it coming." During decades of Cold War, the U.S. often dismissed the factor of nationalism, preferring to see revolutions as instigated by, and partnered with, the Soviet Union or China. More bizarre is that this refusal to recognize the primacy of

[47] See Kevin Baker, "Stabbed in the Back!" *Harper's*, June 2006.
[48] Robert Jay Lifton, *Superpower Syndrome: America's Apocalyptic Confrontation with the World* (Nation Books, 2003).

nationalism continued after the Cold War ended. Without Soviet assistance, U.S. strategists reasoned, Iraqi nationalism could be blown away with Saddam Hussein's dictatorship. The previous eight decades of the country's fitful but passionate exploration of nationalism were glossed over, as if the Iraqis would quickly abandon their historical experience for a stock market and Western imports. This was imperial hubris.

• America's elites are always averse to populist politicians or people in the streets weighing in on foreign policy matters. Just as they frequently intermarry, the elites of the military, corporate law firms, and the executive branch are intermingled in a kind of gated community outside of which everyone is made to feel unqualified to venture an opinion. The national security elite enhances the exclusivity of this club with an aura of secrecy and a whiff of gunpowder. It is no wonder, then, that the elites, including the media, ignored the emergence of an antiwar movement as a possible threat to their established narrative of Iraq and the assumption that the Vietnam Syndrome had been put to rest. As late as March 2007, when a sizeable American majority favored a timed withdrawal from Iraq, the *New York Times* described the seventy-plus member congressional Out of Iraq Caucus as having a "fringe image."[49]

The U.S. government's war in Iraq is foundering between two powerful, separate, but interacting currents well

---

[49] Michael Luo, "Antiwar Caucus Wants to Be Heard Now," *New York Times*, March 7, 2007.

beneath the surface of official reality: the Iraqi insurgency and American memories of Vietnam, now returning like a flood in Iraq.

CHAPTER 2

AS RUST DEVOURS STEEL
THE NATURE OF THE IRAQ INSURGENCY

*I believe demolishing Hussein's military power and liberating Iraq
would be a cakewalk.*
   —Ken Adelman, Defense Policy Board, February 2002[1]

We did not see it coming.
   —General John Keane, U.S. Army, on the Iraq insurgency[2]

We might be a vapour, blowing where we listed.
   —T.E. Lawrence, writing of the Arab Revolt he led, 1921[3]

H ow is it that the United States government, with all
its vaunted intelligence assets, "did not see it coming"? It was blinded by its superpower paradigm: A
feeling of superiority in arms, wealth, or religion always car-
ries an underestimate of the Other. It is never admitted that
oppression and underdevelopment might contain the seeds of
durable resistance.

   When the U.S. and Iraqi exiles took over the presidential

---

[1] Ken Adelman, "Cakewalk in Iraq," *Washington Post*, February 13, 2002.
[2] General John Keane, army deputy chief of staff, Operation Enduring Freedom,
testimony to U.S. House Armed Services Committee, 2004. See Stephen J.
Hedges, "Former U.S. General Says U.S. Military Didn't Expect Iraqi Insurgency," Knight Ridder, July 15, 2004.
[3] Thomas Edward Lawrence, *Seven Pillars of Wisdom* (Wordsworth Editions,
1997), p. 186.

palaces of Saddam Hussein in 2003, they became illegitimate occupiers. Since then, the war has been primarily between Americans trying to turn military power into legitimate authority and insurgents who can defeat their superpower occupiers simply by not surrendering.

According to the CIA, insurgencies are designed to "weaken government control and legitimacy"[4]; the 2006 draft *U.S. Army Field Manual* echoes that an insurgency is "aimed at the overthrow of a constituted government through the use of subversion and armed conflict."[5] But the Iraqi government installed by the U.S. was only "in control" or "constituted" in official rhetoric. It sought to constitute itself, and win control of Iraq, from inside a Green Zone that was a combination of fortress and amusement park. To the average Iraqi, the regime represented collaboration with foreign occupiers. The U.S. government thought it could turn the facts upside down, claiming that the insurgents were the illegitimate outsiders—the Iraqi "dead-enders" to Donald Rumsfeld, in their "last throes" to Vice President Cheney.[6]

Yet the U.S. might have been able to achieve a coerced legitimacy. Weakened severely by a decade of sanctions, the battered Iraqi people might have acquiesced to the new power on the banks of the Tigris, or waited patiently for their new government to provide security and stability. Here lies a great question: *Why didn't they?*

In searching for answers, I am guided by many years as an Irish-American observer of the insurgency and peace talks in Northern Ireland. Both Iraq and Ireland were occupied and colonized by Britain in 1920. In both cases, the British rul-

[4] *Guide to the Analysis of Insurgency* (Central Intelligence Agency, 1986), p. 2.
[5] *U.S. Army Field Manual*, Final Draft (FMI) 3–24, Counterinsurgency (Headquarters, Department of the Army, June 2006), 1–1.
[6] Transcript, *NewsHour with Jim Lehrer*, June 23, 2005.

ers were careful to sort and divide the colonized according to religion and geography. Both countries experienced continual insurgencies, with British forces retreating behind curtains of indirect control through religious minorities (Sunni in the former, Protestant and loyalist in the latter). Britain claimed that both invasions and occupations were necessary to prevent sectarian strife from descending into civil war. But Britain was never a neutral arbiter; it funded, trained, and armed one side in the conflicts. Nevertheless, Sinn Féin and the Irish Republican Army (IRA) were able to battle British forces for thirty years in a province no larger than Iraq's "Sunni Triangle," creating a military stalemate that finally required a political settlement. While Iraq achieved limited sovereignty in 1932, it was not until the British-backed Hashemite monarchy fell in a nationalist coup in 1958 that it could be properly considered an independent state.

The British sent many of their best commanders from Belfast to Baghdad and Basra when the Iraq War began in 2003.[7] They brought with them a counterinsurgency repertoire, inspired by the low-intensity warfare doctrines of Frank Kitson that had been developed in campaigns from Kenya to Malaysia. Kitson had suggested that "conditions can be made reasonably uncomfortable for the population as a whole, in order to provide an incentive for a return to normal life."[8]

In Derry, Northern Ireland, this meant the killing of fourteen Irish civilians by British troops and a subsequent coverup which lasted for three decades. In Basra, an Iraqi hotel receptionist died of ninety-three injuries sustained

[7] See, for example, "The Roles of Engagement: Lessons from Northern Ireland Serve British Troops Well," *Seattle Times*, April 4, 2003.
[8] Frank Kitson, *Low-Intensity Operations: Subversion, Insurgency, and Peacekeeping* (Faber and Faber, 1971), p. 87.

during several days of British custody in late 2003.[9] Curiously, the most senior British Army officer at the time of the Iraq invasion was General Mike Jackson, who had denied allegations that he witnessed his own men shoot civilians in Derry in 1972.[10]

Besides imposing suffering on the "population as a whole," as with sanctions or martial law, the key challenge in Ireland was making the nationalists think that living under colonial rule was part of a "normal life." (I remember Martin McGuinness, an IRA leader and later a negotiator with the British, scoffing in 1976 that "they want to make us Sunday golfers.")

The American plan for the Middle East similarly sought to impose a new pro-Western identity on Arabs, by using everything from overwhelming force, counterintelligence programs, propaganda, new textbooks, consumer imports, Bibles, and candy for the children. It was very familiar.

The Iraq Insurgency[11] as a Social Movement: The Origins

There was a brief moment when American troops felt welcome in Iraq, and Pacifica reporter Aaron Glantz was there:

> Almost everyone I met seemed happy that Saddam was gone. Taxi drivers smiled approvingly when they learned I was American . . . children did come up to the American soldiers to give them flowers and, overall, the occupation

[9] Audrey Gillan, "Father Describes Horror of Seeing Son's Body," *Guardian* (U.K.), April 17, 2007.
[10] Richard Norton-Taylor, "Army Chief Questioned Over 'Shot List,'" *Guardian* (U.K.), October 16, 2003.
[11] I will use the terms *insurgency* and *resistance* interchangeably, although the Iraqis use the term *resistance* and the American press and military prefer the label *insurgency*.

seemed quite friendly. At the ice-cream parlor near our apartment, American soldiers regularly lined up among the locals seeking a respite from the summer heat.[12]

Half the Iraqis polled immediately after the fall of Saddam Hussein's regime felt they were being liberated.[13] But the moment was fleeting. Within days, the occupation was stirring feelings of nationalism and distrust among the population, and their desired "return to normal life" meant order, food, electricity, and a sovereign Iraqi government.

The American paradigm was that the insurgency was a top-down spasm by the regime's "dead-enders," a common mainstream view of social movements as contrived and controlled by conspirators. The U.S. military distributed a deck of cards featuring its most-wanted Iraqis, targeting an imagined command-and-control structure of insurgents. But as the most-wanted were captured and killed, the resistance continued to grow. In the months to come, the U.S. would eliminate all but ten of the fifty-five most-wanted godfathers in their mafia model of resistance (three of whom did not appear in the deck), including Saddam Hussein and his two sons. The model was based on the French general's counterinsurgency strategy in the movie *The Battle of Algiers* (1966), in which the Algerian resistance is compared to a tapeworm that must be chopped off at the head. In the film, which is based on real events and is still studied by Pentagon commanders and students of armed resistance, the Algerian leadership structure was destroyed; but two years later a mass uprising forced the French to withdraw.

Social uprisings, of course, have symbolic, titular, and

---

[12] Aaron Glantz, *How America Lost Iraq* (Tarcher/Penguin, 2005), p. 35.
[13] Patrick Cockburn, *The Occupation: War and Resistance in Iraq* (Verso, 2006), p. 107.

bureaucratic leaders. They have organizations and infrastructures, too. Attacks against these leaders and structures can do damage and cause setbacks. But leadership and organization are far more organic to an oppressed culture than the U.S. model recognizes. They are rooted in communities that share common grievances, humiliations, and living memories. Radical resistance can take the form of *networks* that rise from the experiences of these communities. These are not the vertical organizations that prosecutors and military commanders dream about. As Jason Burke writes in *Al-Qaeda: The True Story of Radical Islam*, the organization itself may not even exist as such. The term al-Qaeda refers to a base, a foundation, and, he says, "it can also mean a precept, rule, principle, maxim, formula, method, model, or pattern."[14] Interestingly, the Arabic term also refers to the lowest, broadest base of a cloud formation.

The U.S. apparently believed that after a brief period of looting, Iraqis would settle into the occupation and rapidly return to work under an American-appointed elite, some of whom were flown in from exile. The assumption was that since Saddam was a dictator, no one in their right mind would have loyalty, as such, to his government. Meanwhile, as the city was plunged into chaos (with no government or police to be found), people started taking matters into their own hands. Most were organized only by neighborhoods and tribes, driven by a combination of rage and necessity. It was Northern Ireland, 1969.

Ahmed S. Hashim, William R. Polk, and other commentators agree that the early phase of resistance was ad hoc and unexpected, rather than organized and disciplined. George Packer wrote that it was a "hodgepodge." Ba'athists

---

[14] Jason Burke, *Al-Qaeda: The True Story of Radical Islam* (Penguin, 2004), p. 1.

participated, but were not the primary trigger of the popular resistance.

In April, tens of thousands of Iraqis took to the streets of Baghdad, Mosul, Fallujah, and smaller cities, demanding food and other necessities. The demonstrations were angry but mostly peaceful, spontaneous, and seemingly without formal leadership. On April 19, 2003, the first large demonstration in Baghdad called for an end to occupation and the creation of an Islamic state.[15] That same week, Sunni clerics formed the Association of Muslim Scholars (AMS), led by Dr. Harith al-Dhari, to oppose the occupation—not unlike the black religious leaders who served as legal intermediaries with the underground resistance in apartheid South Africa. Still, according to Hashim, there was a "wait and see" attitude among many Iraqis toward the U.S., as well as calculated and sometimes enthusiastic support from most Shi'a clerics and parties.

On April 28, however, American troops from the 82nd Airborne in Fallujah shot into a relatively peaceful crowd that was demanding food, killing fifteen people and wounding sixty-five.[16] According to an Iraqi elder who was present, the incident started when a teacher complained that her school was being transformed into a military base. An American soldier pinned her to the ground, a crowd gathered, and the lethal confrontation commenced. Consistent with tribal codes, calls for revenge went out after evening prayers the next day. In response to militant but peaceful chants of "God is great!" U.S. forces killed several more people. There were no American casualties. A Western-based Arab journalist who interviewed Fallujah residents

[15] Ahmed S. Hashim, *Insurgency and Counter-insurgency in Iraq* (Cornell University Press, 2006), p. 19.

[16] Hashim, p. 23. See also, Carl Conetta, "Vicious Circle: The Dynamics of Occupation and Resistance in Iraq," Commonwealth Institute Project on Defense Alternatives (Research Monograph 10), May 18, 2005.

wrote, "In retrospect, although the incident barely registered in the Western media, this confrontation was the spark that fanned the flames of the Fallujah insurgency movement."[17]

Canadian reporter Patrick Graham, who spent months in 2003–04 among fighters in Fallujah, found them to be local people connected by clan. They would raise families, carefully observe American soldiers, enjoy films like *Braveheart*, and learn how to wire roadside bombs.

> *At first, I didn't realize [they] were in the resistance. I had expected to be taken to some undisclosed location where paranoid men, their faces hidden behind scarves, would deliver a ten-minute rant against Zionism and the infidels before driving off in Toyota pickups.*
>
> *I didn't anticipate the endless glasses of tea, or Mohammed, with a child sleeping on his lap, telling me that he didn't think Osama bin Laden was a good Muslim.*
>
> *(Mohammed liked Braveheart, he said, because his grandfather had fought the British. "The problems started," he said, "because the British invaded and take the beautiful women and hurt the people. Because of the hard times, they gather weapons and get rid of the spies and traitors, isn't that right?")* [18]

According to Polk, the "first serious military-style attack" by the insurgency against U.S. forces occurred immediately after the shootings in Fallujah, on May 1, 2003.[19] On that day,

---

[17] Zaki Chehab, *Inside the Resistance: The Iraqi Insurgency and the Future of the Middle East* (Nation Books, 2005), p. 17.

[18] Patrick Graham, "Beyond Fallujah: A Year with the Iraqi Resistance," *Harper's*, June 2004.

[19] William R. Polk, *Understanding Iraq: The Whole Sweep of Iraqi History, from Genghis Khan's Mongols to the Ottoman Turks to the British Mandate to the American Occupation* (HarperCollins, 2005), p. 173.

President Bush announced "mission accomplished" on the deck of an aircraft carrier off the American coast.

Where had the resistance come from?

It arose from a collective memory of the past and from an intolerable chaos of the present, causing the rapid, almost natural proliferation of local networks of resistance wherever American forces were found.

The resistance grew from memories of British colonialism reborn in the new American occupation; for example, memories such as the words of the commanding British officer in Baghdad who said in 1917 that "our armies do not come into your cities and lands as conquerors or enemies but as liberators."[20] The resistance was rooted, too, in the lingering memory of the U.S.–U.K. sanctions of the 1990s, when, for example, Secretary of State Madeleine Albright blithely stated that the deaths of hundreds of thousands of Iraqi children from malnutrition was a price worth paying.[21]

Memory is the hidden well of social movements. As Jason Burke writes, "This perception that a belligerent West is set on the humiliation, division, and eventual conquest of the Muslim world is as much a root cause of Muslim violence as relative poverty or government repression."[22]

The intolerable chaos began with the March 20, 2003 invasion itself, in which tens of thousands of Iraqis were killed and injured during 37,000 air attacks that dumped thirteen

---

[20] Cited in Hashim, p. 64.

[21] See Antonia Juhasz, *The Bush Agenda: Invading the World, One Economy at a Time* (HarperCollins, 2006), p. 174. UNICEF estimated that sanctions caused around 500,000 excess mortalities among Iraqi children ages one to five between 1991–98. On *60 Minutes*, reporter Leslie Stahl asked Albright: "We have heard that a half-million children have died. I mean, that's more than died in Hiroshima. I mean, was it worth it?" Albright answered, "I think this is a very hard choice, but the price, we think the price is worth it." Cited in Mahmood Mamdani, *Good Muslim, Bad Muslim: America, the Cold War, and the Roots of Terror* (Pantheon Books, 2004), p. 190.

[22] Burke, p. 188.

thousand cluster munitions (containing two million cluster bomblets) in three weeks, most of them on civilians.[23] Hundreds of thousands of Iraqi soldiers were dismissed without pay, sent home carrying their weapons. Hundreds of state-owned businesses were shut down, alienating merchants and the professional middle class. De-Ba'athification decrees laid off thousands of skilled technicians and civil servants as well as members of the army. In a typical case, one expelled soldier angrily complained that "after twenty-three years of service to the army, during which I wasted my youth, I ended up selling tea on this sidewalk."[24]

At the same time, basic services suddenly collapsed. After one year of occupation, incomes and employment levels had dropped precipitously, and many Iraqis lacked access to sewage systems, clean water, and reliable electricity.[25] By comparison, Saddam's technicians and engineers had taken only a few months to rebuild much of the basic infrastructure of Iraq that had been purposefully targeted during the 1991 Gulf War.[26]

Some blamed American incompetence or service rivalries for this alleged fiasco,[27] but it appeared that the U.S. had little interest in rebuilding the country. Instead, the U.S. was carrying out the "mass privatization" of Iraq's state-owned economy proposed by a consulting firm on a $250 million contract.[28] Far from being disorganized, the American proconsul

---

[23] George McGovern and William R. Polk, *Out of Iraq: A Practical Plan for Withdrawal Now* (Simon & Schuster, 2006), p. 49. See also, *Off Target: The Conduct of the War and Civilian Casualties in Iraq* (Human Rights Watch, December 2003).

[24] Hashim, p. 96.

[25] Hashim, p. 297.

[26] Juhasz, p. 199.

[27] See, for example, Thomas E. Ricks, *Fiasco: The American Military Adventure in Iraq* (Penguin, 2006).

[28] Juhasz, p. 194. The consulting firm was Bearing Point, Inc., of McLean, Virginia, close to CIA headquarters. It was previously known as KPMG LLP, and changed its name in the wake of the Enron/Arthur Andersen corporate scan-

Paul Bremer unleashed 100 executive orders on privatization, de-Ba'athification, and the like. A weakened and dependent Iraq would apparently serve U.S.–U.K. goals. For the first time in decades, American and British oil companies would gain access to Iraq's oil fields. Those fields, and Iraq's oil ministry building, were among the first properties secured by coalition forces, while looting prevailed elsewhere.

Hashim identifies an "identity disenfranchisement" as the key impact of the U.S. assault on Sunni Arabs and other Iraqis bearing the brunt of the invasion. These Iraqis felt themselves to be *sha'ab bidun*, "a people without." It is worth quoting this Naval War College expert's definition at length:

> *Identity crisis stems from a disruption of one's world and milieu and the quest to make sense of the changes by posing the interrelated questions of how you fit in the new world and whether and how you can remake your identity to fit the new circumstances . . . We cannot wish away the role of identity crisis as a grievance and as a prime cause of the insurgency. But we do so because identity is such an intangible commodity.*[29]

Jason Burke, James Gilligan,[30] and Jessica Stern[31] have all emphasized how violence is triggered by shame, disrespect, and humiliation, the very feelings that occupiers and prison guards instill with their policies. Inmates at Abu Ghraib, just

dals. The contract came from the U.S. Agency for International Development (USAID), to be managed by Paul Bremer's Coalition Provisional Authority.
[29] Hashim, pp. 68–9.
[30] James Gilligan, *Violence: Our Deadly Epidemic and Its Causes* (G.P. Putnam, 1996).
[31] Jessica Stern, *Terrror in the Name of God: Why Religious Militants Kill* (Ecco, 2003).

one of the many brutal prison centers in the country, were stripped naked and sexually tormented.

There is a neo-Crusader dimension to the occupation that chafes at Muslim sensibility as well. The Pentagon under-secretary for intelligence, General William Boykin, has repeatedly boasted of the superiority of Christianity over Islam; so did Joseph E. Smith, the Pentagon's inspector general (and executive of private military contractor Blackwater USA), a proud member of the Order of Malta, which was originally formed to defend territories captured by the Crusaders.[32] James Yee, a former U.S. chaplain to Muslim inmates at Guantánamo, recalls the forcing of prisoners to bow to satanic symbols painted on the prison floor, as the guards shouted, "Satan is your god now, not Allah!"[33]

The result of these present and past humiliations is a deep-seated rage that can lead the victim to lash out in vengeance against the oppressor, or in shame against other victims, or in suicidal self-destruction.

Could this all have been averted? Many argued that the invasion was "botched," that the forceful toppling of the Baghdad regime could have been followed by a softer, more respectful approach based on economic development and the swift pullout of U.S. troops. But was it only incompetence that prevented the implementation of this rosy scenario? If so, was the incompetence individualized or the result of bureaucratic turf battles—or was it somehow systemic? These questions may not be entirely answerable, but future analysis will likely suggest that the occupation was mishandled and could have turned out differently. Yet this would ignore the willingness of the U.S. and U.K. to inflict massive suffering on Iraqi civil-

---

[32] Jeremy Scahill, *Blackwater: The Rise of the World's Most Powerful Mercenary Army* (Nation Books, 2007), p. 299.
[33] Interview with Amy Goodman, *Democracy Now!*, May 22, 2006.

ians during the decade of sanctions, and would assume that the U.S. actually wanted to restore and develop Iraq as an independent Arab state. A mentality that drops two million cluster bomblets during the initial invasion period, however, is incapable of subsequently becoming a Peace Corps committed to economic development.

The very approach that the neoconservatives and the Pentagon believed would crush the Iraqis—shock and awe—contributed instead to the traumatic identity crisis at the heart of the insurgency. What was meant to be an "opportunity to de-Arabize Iraq"[34] inflamed a sense of wounded national and Muslim honor among Iraqis across many lines.

In a poem attributed to Saddam Hussein before his execution, he compared the Iraqi resistance to *rust devouring steel*, in a surprisingly insightful metaphor.[35] Rust is the corrosive coating that forms when iron or steel is exposed to air and moisture. The ingredients of resistance, Saddam was suggesting, lay in the very *nature* of Iraq. As such, there is no stopping the process of gradual decay without ending the occupation itself. The analogy is meant as a metaphor, but has literal referents as well, like the corrosive rusting of U.S. tanks, helicopters, and armor exposed to the harsh Iraqi weather. An American offensive in al-Diyala, east of Baghdad, was described as encountering, for example, "an icy downpour [which] turned dirt roads into muck that stuck to boots and wheels like cement and stopped American armored vehicles."[36]

It is noteworthy that T.E. Lawrence (Lawrence of Arabia) drew on similar naturalistic images to describe the Arab revolt he organized for the British against the Ottoman Empire

[34] Hashim, p. 282.
[35] "Saddam Poem: Ba'athists Bloom, Enemy Is Hollow," *International Herald Tribune*, January 4, 2007.
[36] Alexandra Zavis, "Diyala Offensive Gets Caked in Mud," *Los Angeles Times*, January 9, 2007.

during World War I. Lawrence, an exceptional diarist, wrote of three elements in warfare, disputing the classic notion of war as only being the annihilation of one's enemies. First was the "algebraical factor," consisting of a relation of space and force so vast that it would need fortified posts of twenty men every four square miles, requiring the Ottoman forces to use 600,000 troops. This is reminiscent of U.S. General Eric Shinseki's prewar advice (for which he was immediately rep- rimanded) that "hundreds of thousands" of American troops would be needed.[37] Second and third were the "biological fac- tor" and a "psychological element" of ideas, both revolving around intangible dimensions of Arab culture and spirit. The Ottoman Turks would fail by digging trench lines and forti- fications across the vast desert. But Lawrence imagined the Arabs as

> an influence, an idea, a thing intangible, invulnerable, without front or back, driving about like gas . . . [Con- ventional] armies were like plants, immobile, firm-rooted, nourished through long stems to the head. We might be a vapour, blowing where we listed.[38]

Lawrence summarized the military advantages of the "va- pours" of Iraqi resistance in remarkably contemporary terms. The rebellion had an "unassailable base" in its Arab conscious- ness; there was a "sophisticated alien enemy" pinned down in "fortified posts"; the insurgency was backed by "a friendly

[37] Wolfowitz denounced Shinseki's estimate, given in Senate testimony, as "quite outlandish" and "way off the mark." Wolfowitz also declared on Febru- ary 27, 2003 to the House Budget Committee that "one should at least pay attention to past experience." But the army's Center of Military History, which sourced Shinseki's testimony, had looked back only to World War II, apparently not to Lawrence's 1921 diaries. Cited in Ricks, pp. 96–100.

[38] Lawrence, p. 182.

population . . . of which some two in the hundred were active, and the rest quietly sympathetic to the point of not betraying the movements of the minority."[39]

Little has changed since 1921. Those counterinsurgency experts who dream of being modern Lawrences of Arabia forget that the man was promoting an Arab insurrection against the Turks, not asking the Arabs to become vassals of the British.[40]

THE OCCUPATION CAUSES THE INSURGENCY

The U.S. military at first followed the conventional "kinetic" war model in which the prime emphasis is attrition—that is, the destruction of the enemy—rather than a strategy placing priority on reducing popular support for the enemy. As one British critic noted, the U.S. Soldier's Creed reads in part that an army "warrior" stands "ready to deploy, engage, and destroy the enemies of the United States of America in close combat," not merely deter or contain them.[41] A military study of 127 pacification efforts between May 2003 and May 2005 showed that most operations were to "hunt down insurgents," while only six percent "were directed specifically to create a secure environment for the population."[42]

The U.S. was operating under an assumption, inherited from and shared with the British and Israeli governments, that the only language understood by Arabs is force. (I encountered this concept firsthand twenty years ago as I watched the

---

[39] Lawrence, p. 186.
[40] One such dreamer is the Australian David Kilcullen, an influential counterinsurgency expert in U.S. government circles. See George Packer, "Knowing the Enemy," *New Yorker*, December 18, 2006.
[41] Cited in Brigadier Nigel Aylwin-Foster, British Army, "Changing the Army for Counterinsurgency Operations," *Military Review*, November/December 2005, p. 4.
[42] Pentagon's Quadrennial Defense Review, 2006 (U.S. Government Printing Office, May 23, 2005). Also cited in Aylwin-Foster, p. 5.

Israel Defense Forces blow up the family home of a Palestinian terrorist suspect.)

U.S. officials remained supremely confident through 2003, at least outwardly. Besides the president's May 1 pronouncement that "major combat operations in Iraq have ended," neoconservative Reuel Marc Gerecht declared "victory" in the *Weekly Standard* for "the restoration of American awe and the opening of the Arab mind,"[43] which was precisely the opposite of what was happening.

THE FRAGMENTED COMPOSITION OF THE RESISTANCE

As late as December 2006, the Baker-Hamilton Iraq Study Group complained that the U.S. Administration was "not doing enough to map the insurgency, dissect it, and understand it on a national and provincial level." The *ISG Report* noted there were less than ten counterinsurgency analysts at the Defense Intelligence Agency with more than two years' experience.[44] Few American journalists ventured into areas where they could interview the insurgents. Additionally, the Iraqis themselves were well-schooled historically in clandestine organizational techniques. In the 1960s, the U.S. had experienced the same failure to grasp an enemy they called "the faceless Vietcong."

Information was available, however, in works like Hashim's book on the insurgency, while historians Gareth Porter, Robert Fisk, and Robert Dreyfuss, along with journalists Dexter Filkins and Robert Collier, were among the few who attempted to understand the resistance. Excellent studies of the occupation and

[43] Reuel Marc Gerecht, "The Restoration of American Awe," *Weekly Standard*, May 12, 2003.
[44] James A. Baker III and Lee H. Hamilton, cochairs, *The Iraq Study Group Report* (Vintage Books, 2006), p. 94.

resistance have been issued by Carl Conetta at the Project for Defense Alternatives (PDA) in Cambridge, Massachusetts.

It was not until December 2005 that the *New York Times'* Filkins reported what officials in Iraq were finally beginning to admit:

> *The single most important fact about the insurgency is that it consists not of a few groups but of dozens, possibly as many as 100. And it is not, as often depicted, a coherent organization whose members dutifully carry out orders from above, but a far-flung collection of smaller groups that often act on their own or come together for a single attack . . . Each group is believed to have its own leader and is free to act on its own.*[45]

One thing is certain: The resistance is not a unified national liberation movement. It is agreed that the U.S. should leave, but divided by different visions of what Iraq has been and should become.

THE al-QAEDA ALLEGATION

It appears that the Bush Administration invented its own devil in the form of al-Qaeda in Iraq. While journalists, historians, and commissions have discredited allegations that Saddam Hussein collaborated with al-Qaeda, the 2003 invasion itself became a magnet for foreign jihadists to migrate to Iraq, and they eventually formed an entity known as al-Qaeda in Mesopotamia. This insurgent group has attracted some Iraqis to its original cadre of Saudis, Jordanians, and Palestinians. But it also is true that foreign presence was "miniscule," as

[45] Dexter Filkins, "Profusion of Rebel Groups Helps Them Survive in Iraq," *New York Times*, December 2, 2005.

Hashim points out—of 8,000 detainees in Iraq in 2004, for example, just 127 held foreign passports.[46]

An Israeli study of the profiles of 154 captured foreign fighters concluded that the vast majority never took part in terrorist activity prior to entering Iraq—i.e., they were not hardened operatives arriving from previous battlegrounds.[47] *The ISG Report* endorsed the view that "al-Qaeda is responsible for only a small portion of the violence in Iraq," although its attacks are often spectacular. The report estimated about 1,300 "foreign fighters" in Iraq,[48] fewer than the Abraham Lincoln Brigades during the Spanish Civil War.

Al-Qaeda's presence was a direct result of the American invasion, not the other way around, which suggests that the departure of American troops would shrink its base among ordinary Iraqis fighting for nationalist reasons. By 2006, al-Qaeda became mired in a nasty ideological war against another Sunni group in al-Anbar province that had American funding and weapons. This would evolve into a protracted civil conflict among Sunnis themselves.

The Sunni Armed Resistance

The overall resistance is fragmented along fault lines that reach back to the days when the British groomed and elevated the Sunnis as their collaborating class. When the Ba'athists later took power, Saddam's party and state became Arab nationalist in character (though not entirely in membership) and was dominated by a Sunni elite. Therefore, it is no surprise that the Sunni community is the strongest supporter of today's resistance to the occupation, seeking to preserve

[46] Hashim, p. 139.
[47] Hashim, pp. 150–1.
[48] *The Iraq Study Group Report*, p. 4.

Iraq as a unitary Arab state beyond Saddam. The Sunnis are a large majority in al-Anbar province to the west of Baghdad, across the Sunni Triangle region, and until recently in large swaths of Baghdad. Polk estimates that Sunnis number twenty to thirty percent of the roughly sixteen to twenty million Iraqi Arabs.[49]

The Sunni insurgency includes both secular members (usually former Ba'athists) and Islamic hardliners, who are represented through groups like the Association of Muslim Scholars. One key difference exists between those fighting to expel the U.S. and rebuild a nationalist state and those who see Iraq as one front in a wider jihad against Western imperialism: The vast majority of insurgent fighters belong to the first camp, primarily identify themselves as Iraqi, and have vowed that, if necessary, they will take up arms to quell the jihadists after American forces leave. Hashim's 2006 book identified nineteen separate insurgent groups, most of them Sunni in background.[50]

THE SHI'A AGENDA: U.S. OCCUPATION TODAY, ISLAMIC REPUBLIC TOMORROW

Most, though not all, of the Shi'a majority (which numbers at least sixty percent of the population) are engaged in a liberation movement from past Sunni rule, and have accepted the U.S. as a *temporary* ally against the former Ba'ath regime. They pressured the U.S. to hold the elections which brought the Shi'a majority to power. This made the Shi'a appear to the Sunnis as collaborators with the U.S., even among Sunnis who had suffered under Saddam. The Shi'a, on the other hand, have seen the American presence as a shield against

[49] Polk, *Understanding Iraq*, p. 6.
[50] Hashim, p. 170.

the return of the old regime, but most do not desire a permanent occupation of their country. In surveys, the large majority of Shi'a oppose the occupation and want a U.S. withdrawal timetable, though not by as large a percentage as the Sunnis.

The Shi'a are divided along class and identity lines, as well as by attitudes toward the U.S. occupation. The Ayatollah Ali al-Sistani, who is Iranian by birth, seeks to maximize the unity of the Shi'a coalition for purposes of wielding power, and is the leader that the U.S. most depends upon (though no American has ever met him). The Dawa Party, formed in the late 1950s, is the base of Iraq's current prime minister, Nouri al-Maliki, and suffered greatly under Saddam as a clandestine movement. The Supreme Council for the Islamic Revolution in Iraq (SCIRI) was established in Iran during the early 1980s. Its leadership, centered around the al-Hakim family, represents the "commercial middle class who had managed to go into exile in the relative safety of Iran."[51] Its militia, the Badr Brigade, can be characterized as an anti-Sunni, anti-Ba'athist organization functioning as Shi'a neighborhood security forces, death squads, and as the core element of the Iraqi Interior Ministry. Politically, SCIRI favors an Iraq closely allied to Iran that would have an autonomous Shi'a-controlled region (a Shi'astan, similar to Kurdistan) in the oil-laden south, a development which is well underway.

Then there is the Mahdi Army,[52] led by Muqtada al-Sadr, often described in the American media as the most dangerous, powerful, and popular individual in Iraq[53]—phrases which

---

[51] Hashim, p. 267.

[52] *Mahdi* is a reference to the Hidden Imam of Shi'a Islam, whose return, according to adherents of the Twelver Shi'a branch, will happen at the end time.

[53] Jeffrey Bartholet, "How al-Sadr May Control U.S. Fate in Iraq." *Newsweek* published this cover story, a virtual hit piece on December 4, 2006, with a black headline over a red cover screaming, *The Most Dangerous Man in Iraq*, complete with a photo of the menacing cleric striding forward in a martial style.

usually hint of a coming assassination or removal, scenarios which have already been attempted.[54]

Al-Sadr is the leading Shi'a demanding an immediate U.S. withdrawal deadline, setting him at odds with al-Sistani and al-Hakim.[55] Al-Sadr is not only prominent for leading mass mobilizations against the occupation, but also for capturing thirty seats in the Iraqi Parliament. His core constituents, who number two million in Sadr City, the slums of eastern Baghdad, especially valued his control of the health and transportation portfolios, which he voluntarily relinquished in April 2007. These are a people so undernourished that many thousands have been stunted physically and mentally for lack of basic food and medicine. Their class differences with the SCIRI constituency are palpable depite religious commonalities. Situated in Baghdad without oil resources, they would not be served by partition and the creation of an autonomous SCIRI-controlled region in the south.

It is from these ranks that al-Sadr built his militia, which serves to provide armed security and distribute food and social services in neighborhoods that would otherwise be overlooked. (In this regard, it can be compared to the Black Panther Party.) Twice in 2004 the Mahdi Army rose up against U.S. forces, and has at times expressed support and solidarity for Sunni insurgents in Fallujah, creating a scene similar to the British nightmare of the 1920 Sunni–Shi'a joint uprising.

[54] The U.S. planned to forcibly arrest al-Sadr in 2003, making sure "it was not seen as an American operation," according to a Rumsfeld memo. A top U.S. official argued that "we should take down Sadr now, when no one's looking" (Bartholet, *Newsweek*, December 4, 2006). Since that time, the U.S. military has sought permission to capture or kill al-Sadr on various occasions.

[55] Al-Sadr led 10,000 demonstrators carrying placards demanding *No to foreign administration* and *Yes to Islam* on May 19, 2003, insisting that an elected government replace the U.S. and its foreign-based Iraqi allies. See Larry Jay Diamond, *Squandered Victory: The American Occupation and the Bungled Effort to Bring Democracy to Iraq* (Owl Books, 2006), p. 37.

On the fourth anniversary of the fall of Baghdad to U.S. forces, al-Sadr staged a massive protest in Najaf calling for an end to the occupation. Days later, he ordered his six representatives in the Iraqi cabinet to quit the government, putting further pressue on Prime Minister al-Maliki to demand the exit of foreign troops. As the *New York Times* reported, al-Sadr "was withdrawing his ministers from the 38-member cabinet because the Iraqi government had refused to set a timetable for pulling American troops out of the country."[56] (Al-Sadr has indicated that he will for now leave his thirty parliamentary representatives in government.)

The Mahdi Army is not the only Shi'a party favoring withdrawal; there is also the al-Fadhila party, led by Nadim al-Jabiri, with fifteen seats in Parliament. Al-Sadr and al-Jabiri are Shi'a Arab nationalists, and efforts to demonize and isolate them cannot cloud the fact of their popularity: In September 2006, a survey of 501 Iraqi Shi'a found that sixty-three percent supported attacks against Americans and eighty percent of Baghdad's Shi'a demanded U.S. withdrawal within one year.[57]

Al-Sadr is anti–U.S. occupation and also resents the historical Persian (Iranian) dominance of Shi'ism; further, he distinguishes between nationalist Sunnis and other Sunnis he labels "Saddamis" and *nawasib* (Sunnis who have a violent hatred of Shi'a).[58] Hence, he may be capable of forming a de facto coalition with certain Sunni nationalists to expel the U.S. and bring about a new distribution of power in Baghdad. In 2005, he mediated a violent dispute between the (Sunni)

---

[56] Edward Wong, "Ministers Loyal to Iraqi Cleric Quit Government Posts," *New York Times*, April 16, 2007.

[57] Poll conducted by WorldPublicOpinion.org, cited in Bartholet, *Newsweek*, December 4, 2006.

[58] Juan Cole, "Muqtada al-Sadr and the Sunnis," *Informed Comment*, January 4, 2007 (http://www.juancole.com/2007_01_01_juanricole_archive.html).

Association of Muslim Scholars and the (Shi'a) SCIRI coalition.[59] He has also explored a strategic relationship with the
Sunni National Dialogue Front. In early 2007, veteran Iraq
correspondent Robert Collier quoted al-Sadr as saying that if
he was an ayatollah he would issue a *fatwa* on any sectarian
violence against those he called (Sunni) "brothers."[60]

In summary, only sectarian divisions, and any forces promoting those divisions, prevent sufficient Shi'a–Sunni unity
toward expelling American forces. Whether intentional or
not, divide-and-conquer is the underlying thrust of U.S. policy
against this popular threat.

THE KURDISH WEDGE

The ancient mountainous lands of the Kurds are spread across
Turkey, Iran, and the northeast corner of Iraq, in slices carved
by the British in the aftermath of World War I. The British
colonial adviser Gertrude Bell convinced Winston Churchill
to annex "Kurdistan" into Iraq in an attempt to balance the
population against the Shi'a in the 1920s.[61] While the historic
oppression of the Kurdish people is legendary, it goes beyond
the scope of these pages. The key issue is that the Kurds are
an explosive force in the divisions that are currently bleeding
Iraq. They were allies in the 2003 U.S. invasion, have lived
under U.S.–U.K. protection since the 1990s, and have some
strategic links with Israel. Their *peshmerga* have participated
alongside Iraqi security forces against the insurgency. Seeking to maximize their autonomy as a twenty percent minority
within the Iraqi state, they may now be on a military collision

[59] Cole, "Muqtada al-Sadr and the Sunnis," *Informed Comment*.
[60] Robert Collier, "Talks with Radicals Called Key to Ending Violence," *San Francisco Chronicle*, January 7, 2007.
[61] Peter W. Galbraith, *The End of Iraq: How American Incompetence Created a War Without End* (Simon & Schuster, 2006), p. 151.

course with other Iraqis over the control of oil resources in Kirkuk.

Overall the Kurds provide crucial votes supporting the governing coalition, though they may not be able to gain uni-lateral control of Kirkuk in any scenario. They will continue to press for de facto autonomy, angling for domestic political advantage while observing caution to avoid provoking an in-vasion from Turkey, which fears its own restive Kurdish mi-nority population.

The Kurdish wedge serves as a pivotal factor making the restoration of a strong Iraqi state virtually impossible. The Kurds will never willingly return to a second-class position in Iraq. Most will oppose any American troop withdrawals, and might even provide basing rights in the north when the U.S. departs from the rest of Iraq.

THE HIDDEN FACTOR OF IRAQI PUBLIC OPINION

While the media has been apologetic about its lack of criti-cal independence during the buildup to war, its continu-ing support of the official *political* narrative in Iraq is rarely mentioned. In this spin, the Iraqis need U.S. forces for na-tion-building, regardless of whether the 2003 invasion was mistaken or mishandled. The media reinforces the notion that after "democratic elections," the Iraqi state now rep-resents the Iraqi people, and must therefore be nourished and protected. The single greatest failure of the media in this conflict has been its reluctance to report Iraqi public opinion.

As the historic Iraqi elections approached in January 2005, U.S. intelligence operatives reported that the new gov-ernment would "almost certainly ask the United States to set a specific timetable for withdrawing its troops." The Iraqis leading the majority coalition "promised voters they will press Washington for a timetable for withdrawal, and assessments say the new Iraqi government will feel bound, at least publicly, to meet that commitment." This intelligence report reflected a "grim tone," for it meant the U.S. would have to prevent the very government it had created from carrying out its mandate.[62]

The U.S. government has continued on this course, even after 131 of 275 Iraqi parliamentarians signed another call for a withdrawal timetable as recently as December 2006.[63] Over a year earlier, in June 2005, one-third of the Parliament signed a similar petition for withdrawal, and in September 2005, the eighteen-member Iraqi National Sovereignty Committee voted unanimously for the withdrawal of what it called "the occupation forces." The only major American media reporting this event was Knight Ridder.[64] In November 2005, 100 Sunni, Shi'a, and Kurdish leaders also demanded a timetable at a Cairo conference hosted by the Arab League.[65]

Containing Iraqi majority opinion has been a primary goal of the occupation all along. Various surveys show that Iraqi public support for the resistance has risen steadily since 2003.[66] During April 2003, Iraqis were sharply divided, with forty-six percent calling the U.S. "occupiers" and forty-three

[62] Douglas Jehl, "U.S. Intelligence Says Iraqis Will Press for Withdrawal," *New York Times*, January 19, 2005.

[63] Sudarsan Raghavan, "Shiite Clerics' Rivalry Deepens in Fragile Iraq," *Washington Post*, December 21, 2006.

[64] Nancy Youssef, "Calling U.S. Troops 'Occupation Forces,' Iraqis Seek Timetable for Exit," Knight Ridder, September 13, 2005.

[65] Hassan M. Fattah, "Iraqi Factions Seek Timetable for U.S. Pullout," *New York Times*, November 22, 2005.

[66] Most of these statistics for 2004–05 were compiled by Carl Conetta, "What Do Iraqis Want? Iraqi Attitudes on Occupation, U.S. Withdrawal, Iraqi Governments, and Quality of Life," Commonwealth Institute Project on Defense Alternatives, February 1, 2005.

percent calling them "liberators." Those numbers shifted to 67-15 by October 15, only six months later.[67]

In February 2004, forty percent favored an American withdrawal after an Iraqi government was in place; thirty-three percent wanted withdrawal within one year; twenty-seven percent preferred a longer presence.[68] In March–April 2004, fifty-seven percent said the U.S. should "leave immediately," while thirty-six percent preferred its forces to "stay longer."[69] In a June 2004 Coalition Provisional Authority poll, forty-one percent called for "immediate wihdrawal" and forty-five percent demanded withdrawal after elections.[70]

By January 2005, according to Zogby, eighty-two percent of Sunni Arabs and sixty-nine percent of Shi'a favored U.S. withdrawal "either immediately or after an elected government is in place."[71] Those percentages have remained stable.

Regarding attacks on U.S. troops: In March–April 2004, thirty percent said attacks were somewhat or completely justified, while twenty-two percent said they were sometimes justified.[72] In December 2005, forty-one percent said attacks were justified.[73] In January 2006, Knight Ridder reported that forty-seven percent of Iraqis supported attacks on American troops, including eighty-eight percent of Sunnis, forty-one percent of Shi'a, and sixteen percent of Kurds. Seventy percent supported a timetable for withdrawal, with half favoring

[67] Poll conducted by Iraq's Centre for Research and Strategic Studies. Cited in Patrick Cockburn, "Wolfowitz Survives Hotel Rocket Attack," *Independent* (U.K.), October 27, 2003.
[68] Oxford Research International polls, February/June 2004. Cited in Conetta, "What Do Iraqis Want?"
[69] Gallup/CNN/*USA Today* poll, April 2004. Cited in Conetta.
[70] Independent Institute for Administration and Civil Society/CPA poll, May 2004. Cited in Conetta.
[71] Zogby poll, January 2005. Cited in Conetta.
[72] Gallup/CNN/*USA Today* poll, April 2004. Cited in Conetta.
[73] Drew Brown, "Nearly Half of Iraqis Support Attacks on U.S. Troops, Poll Finds," Knight Ridder, January 31, 2006.

a six-month timeline and half leaning toward two years. In September 2006, as noted, even sixty-three percent of Shi'a supported attacks on U.S. troops.[74]

Overall, of 1,711 Iraqis interviewed in October–November 2005, a majority of sixty-five percent opposed the presence of coalition forces (with forty-four percent "strongly opposed") and fifty-nine percent felt the U.S. military had done a bad job (forty percent a "very bad job").

Regarding views of their own country, Iraqis are divided along ethnic and religious lines. In December 2005, several news organizations asked, "What do Iraqis really want?" and found that eight-five percent of Sunnis opposed U.S. forces; only twenty-five percent felt life was better since the war; thirty-six percent approved of the new constitution; and only sixteen percent felt the U.S. was right to invade.[75] Fifty-nine percent of Shi'a felt life was better, yet fifty-nine percent also opposed the U.S. coalition. Baghdad's residents felt life was better by fifty-nine percent, but opposed the coalition forces by seventy-two percent. Only the Kurds were pleased with the situation, with seventy-three percent feeling life was better and only twenty-two percent opposing the U.S. forces.

Disillusionment ran very deep. Eighty percent of Iraqis believe that the U.S. plans to keep permanent bases in the country after withdrawal.

With this degree of public sympathy, the Iraqi resistance seems to be capable of sustaining itself. It is likely that the Iraqi insurgency has greater popular support than the American colonists' resistance to British rule 250 years before. Many historians agree with John Adams's estimate that the revolution against the British in 1776 succeeded with only one-third of the colonists in support and one-third still loyal

[74] WorldOpinion.org poll, cited in Bartholet, *Newsweek*, December 4, 2006.
[75] *Time*/ABC News poll, December 19, 2005.

to London.[76] Those who say the violence between Iraqis is greater than that toward the U.S. military are forgetting that most of the fighting during the American Revolution occurred between the colonists. According to Ray Raphael, there was "more antagonism toward the Tories than toward the British," and proportionately more colonists fled America between 1775–85 than royalists fled from the French Revolution.[77]

In other words, no level of sectarian conflict can change the fact that the country is generally united against the occupation. As a result, there is ample public sympathy to maintain the resistance for as long as necessary. Dexter Filkins and David Cloud of the *New York Times* concluded in mid-2005: "They just keep getting stronger."[78]

LEVELS OF INSURGENT VIOLENCE INCREASE IN 2006

U.S. propagandists assert that the war cannot be lost militarily, on the battlefield, but only at home, politically. The point is to blame domestic public opinion, the media, the Democratic Party, the "enemy within," anyone except the warmakers themselves. But it is never mentioned that the war is being lost politically *in Iraq*, not against masked guerrillas but on the battlefield of public opinion. There is nothing inherent in being a superpower that guarantees victory in a war against an enemy with popular support and will. The Vietnam War ended with the U.S.-backed client regime imploding and sur-

[76] Howard Zinn, A *People's History of the United States: 1492–Present* (Harper-Collins, 2001), p. 77. See also, Ray Raphael, A *People's History of the American Revolution* (New Press, 2002), p. 217.
[77] Richards, p. 172, 178. During 1775–85, approximately 80,000–100,000 Americans left the country for political reasons. Richards writes: "As a percentage of the overall population, this was five to six times the displacement created by the French Revolution."
[78] Dexter Filkins and David S. Cloud, *New York Times*, July 24, 2005, "Defying U.S. Efforts, Guerrillas in Iraq Refocus and Strengthen."

rendering. Who can say whether the same fate awaits the U.S.-backed government in the Green Zone?

It is also true, on the other hand, that the armed resistance might someday be worn down militarily and divided internally enough to fade away, as some claim happened with British counterinsurgency operations in Malaysia during the early '60s. The widely mentioned "Malaysia model" required a force of 300,000 colonial troops against 9,000 insurgents, and a biased colonial media that effectively kept any coverage of its brutality from British or global purview.[79] U.S. generals estimate that defeating all the major factions of the Iraqi insurgency will take a "few more years," usually defined as three, five, seven, or longer. That U.S. timetable may not be sustainable, but even if it is, what would such a "victory" entail? Surely not the erasure of Iraqi nationalism or Islamic identity. There would be police-state controls, led by American forces, clamped on a permanently hostile population too weary to continue armed resistance.

Yet by nearly every indicator, the armed resistance is growing more effective rather than wearing down.

Steady attacks by guerrilla fighters threaten Iraq's access to electricity. In July 2006, guerrillas successfully attacked *all* the country's fifteen critical power lines along a 2,500-mile network, after previously attacking just two or three at a time. Before the war, Baghdad had sixteen to twenty-four hours of power daily, an average that has declined to 6.6 hours by optimistic estimates. The *New York Times* reported in December 2006 that the "insurgents have effectively won their battle to

[79] See Milton Osborne, "Getting the Job Done, Iraq and the Malayan Emergency," Lowy Institute, February 2005; the Malay insurgents were led by the Communist Party of the Chinese ethnic minority against the ethnic Malay police. This might parallel the dynamic in Iraq, where the primary insurgencies are rooted in the Sunni minority, but as noted, most Shi'a oppose the foreign occupation.

bring down critical high-voltage lines and cut off the capital from the major power plants to the north, south, and west."[80]

On the same day that Robert M. Gates replaced Donald Rumsfeld as defense secretary, the Pentagon's quarterly assessment of security in Iraq noted 960 attacks per week against Americans and Iraqis, a twenty-two percent increase from the previous quarter. Civilian deaths and injuries had reached a record ninety-three per day.[81]

According to Pentagon data, weekly attacks since April 2004 have been steadily increasing:

- just under 400 weekly attacks during April–June 2004;
- above 400 weekly from June–November 2004;
- dipping just below 400 weekly during November–February 2005;
- climbing over 400 weekly again by August 2005–February 2006;
- jumping to 500 weekly in May–August 2006;
- exceeding 600 weekly during August–November 2006.
- In addition to daily attacks doubling in the first six months of 2006, the number of roadside bombs, either discovered or exploded, also increased from 1,415 in January to 2,625 in July.[82]

"The insurgency has gotten worse by almost all measures, with insurgent attacks at historically high levels. The insur-

[80] James Glanz, "Iraq Insurgents Starve Capital of Electricity," *New York Times*, December 19, 2006.
[81] "Measuring Stability and Security in Iraq," Department of Defense, November 2006.
[82] Michael R. Gordon, Mark Mazzetti, and Thom Shanker, "Bombs Aimed at GIs in Iraq Are Increasing," *New York Times*, August 17, 2006.

gency has more public support and is demonstrably more capable in numbers of people active and in its ability to direct violence than at any point in time," said an unnamed Pentagon official in August 2006.[83]

THE SECTARIAN CIVIL WAR

I hope they kill each other . . . Too bad they both can't lose.
—Henry Kissinger, commenting on the
Iraq–Iran war in the 1980s[84]

We will . . . turn them one against another . . .
—President George W. Bush, address to Congress,
September 20, 2001

We sit back and watch because that can only benefit us.
—Lieutenant Colonel Steven Miska, deputy commander of the Dagger Brigade Combat Team in western Baghdad, on insurgent groups fighting one another, December 2006[85]

The term "civil war" was introduced into mainstream discourse in 2006, but only after months of Pentagon and White House denials and pressure on the media. It was feared that "civil war" represented mission failure and would feed the rising domestic criticism. While there was intense sectarian violence, I will use the term "civil war" with a major disclaimer: It is too simple to describe the situation in Iraq as a civil war when the United States is fully funding and propping up one

---

[83] "Bombs Aimed at GIs in Iraq Are Increasing," *New York Times*, August 17, 2006.
[84] Cited in Barry Lando, *Web of Deceit: The History of Western Complicity in Iraq, from Churchill to Kennedy to George W. Bush* (Other Press, 2007), p. 48.
[85] Marc Santora, "Sectarian Ties Weaken Duty's Call for Iraq Forces," *New York Times*, December 28, 2006.

side. Although Iraq has steadily deteriorated into civil war since March 2003, there was certainly no such civil war before the invasion. The Sunni insurgents began attacking Shi'a not on religious grounds—though historic sectarian conflicts were present—but because so many Shi'a were perceived as collaborating with American neocolonial power structures.

While much has been written about the military aspects of the neoconservatives' "Project for the New American Century," little mention is made of the divide-and-conquer strategies intended to break up Arab nationalism, partition the Middle East, bolster Israel, and privatize the region's economies. An excellent book on the history of these strategies is Robert Dreyfuss's *Devil's Game*, which traces the hidden affinities of the CIA, Mossad, and other Western Machiavellians for Islamic fundamentalists against Arab nationalism and Marxism.[86] A prime example of the inherent volatility of this strategy was the U.S. funding and arming of the Afghan mujahideen against the Soviet Union during the 1980s. President Carter's National Security Adviser Zbigniew Brzezinski claimed that the Cold War goal of defeating the Soviet Union was more important in world history than the risks involved with the U.S. giving arms and support to "some agitated Muslims."[87] One outcome of this support was the maturing of al-Qaeda.

A leading Arabist in American policy circles, Bernard Lewis is a former British intelligence officer and was a key adviser to the late Senator Henry "Scoop" Jackson, the hero of the Democratic Party's faction of Cold War hawks who became the neoconservatives. Lewis proposed the dismemberment of Arab nationalism at the time of the first Gulf War:

[86] Robert Dreyfuss, *Devil's Game: How the United States Helped Unleash Fundamentalist Islam* (Metropolitan Books, 2005).
[87] Cited in *Le Nouvel Observateur*, Paris, January 15–21, 1998.

If the central power is sufficiently weakened, there is no real civil society to hold the polity together, no real sense of common identity . . . The state then disintegrates—as happened in Lebanon—into a chaos of squabbling, feuding, fighting sects, tribes, regions, and parties.[88]

A similar policy was supported by the former director-general of the Israeli Foreign Ministry, Shlomo Avineri. In a 2005 op-ed piece entitled "Israel Could Live with a Fractured, Failed Iraq," he wrote: "An Iraq split into three semi-autonomous mini-states, or an Iraq in civil war, means that the kind of threat posed by Hussein . . . is unlikely to arise again."[89] During the run-up to the invasion, Israeli generals—who were described as "routinely" visiting the Pentagon—made a point of wanting to dismantle "what was once the most powerful Arab army on their doorstep."[90]

Other neoconservatives went further. Richard Perle and former George W. Bush speechwriter David Frum suggested supporting independence for the Shi'a of eastern Saudi Arabia, the heart of the kingdom's oil fields.[91] Reuel Marc Gerecht, a former CIA agent and fellow at the American Enterprise Institute, advised that America's "most valuable potential democratic allies" in the Middle East were hardline Islamic believers rather than liberals and moderates, even advocating the support of the Muslim Brotherhood in Egypt.[92]

All of these seemingly paradoxical arguments by neocon-

[88] Bernard Lewis, "Rethinking the Middle East," *Foreign Affairs*, Fall 1992.

[89] Shlomo Avineri, "Israel Could Live with a Fractured, Failed Iraq," *Los Angeles Times*, December 4, 2005.

[90] Mark Fineman, Warren Vieth, and Robin Wright, "Dissolving Iraqi Army Was Costly Choice," *Los Angeles Times*, August 24, 2003.

[91] See Richard Perle and David Frum, *An End to Evil: How to Win the War on Terror* (Random House, 2003).

[92] Reuel Marc Gerecht, *The Islamic Paradox: Shiite Clerics, Sunni Fundamen-*

servatives rest on an unremitting hostility to secular Arab nationalism as exemplified by Egypt's late president Gamal Abdel Nasser, the PLO's Yasser Arafat, and, most recently, Saddam Hussein. Of course, while they have little love for the alternative—the Shi'a fundamentalism on display in Iran, southern Lebanon, Sadr City, and Basra—the American invasion and occupation of Iraq has depended on the acceptance of the Grand Ayatollah al-Sistani and other influential Shi'a clerics. The de facto alliance between the White House and the ayatollahs may strengthen if Iraq provides military bases and oil rights to the U.S. in exchange for protection against Sunni discontent in the region.

It is important to relate these divide-and-conquer approaches to the strategic goals of the U.S. in the Middle East. An American victory in Iraq would reduce the influence of OPEC, which is dominated by Saudi Arabia, and provide U.S. military basing options in Iraq as an alternative to dependence on Saudi Arabia. "We would be much more in a position of strength vis-à-vis the Saudis," said Patrick Clawson, deputy director of the Washington Institute for Near East Policy.[93]

Subdividing Iraq has been promoted by influential diplomats such as Leslie Gelb, the president emeritus of the Council on Foreign Relations; Peter Galbraith, the former ambassador to Croatia and longtime lobbyist for the Kurds; John Yoo, the Bush Justice Department official who wrote the notorious memos defending torture[94]; and Senator Joseph Biden, a 2008 Democratic presidential candidate. Instead of encouraging democratically elected governments in the Middle East, the

talists, and the Coming of Arab Democracy (AEI Press, 2004), p. 18. See also, Dreyfuss, pp. 340–1.
[93] John Donnelly and Anthony Shadid, "Iraq War Hawks Have Plans to Reshape Entire Middle East," Boston Globe, September 10, 2002.
[94] John Yoo, "A United Iraq—What's the Point?" Los Angeles Times, August 25, 2005.

hawks began to claim that partition was *inevitable*, that the Kurds were already flying their own flag, that the Shi'a would get "some form of Islamic republic."[95] The Sunnis would have to end their resistance and accept second-class status, or face a military assault from U.S. troops and Shi'a militias.

As 2006 ended, the ethnic cleansing of Sunnis from Baghdad was the reality behind the rhetoric of civil war. "District by District, Shiites Make Baghdad Their Own," the *New York Times* reported. Ten mixed neighborhoods were "almost entirely Shiite" one year after the Shi'a took power.[96] The *International Herald Tribune* described Sunni enclaves as "withering into abandoned ghettos, starved of government services."[97] The Baghdad provincial council, in charge of all services, included only one Sunni among its fifty-one members.[98] One American expert favored expediting "voluntary ethnic relocation" with housing and job assistance to those facing violent ethnic cleansing.[99] Even National Security Adviser Stephen Hadley admitted in a leaked memo that the regime was carrying out a "campaign to consolidate Shi'a power in Baghdad."[100]

The new model proposed by President Bush in January 2007 involved subdividing Baghdad into what was promoted literally as "gated communities": After sweeping all suspected insurgents out of the areas, the military would create con-

[95] Robin Wright and Ellen Knickmeyer, "U.S. Lowers Sights on What Can Be Achieved in Iraq," *Washington Post*, August 14, 2005.

[96] Sabrina Tavernise, Hosham Hussein, and Qais Mizher, "District by District, Shiites Make Baghdad Their Own," *New York Times*, December 23, 2006.

[97] Damien Cave, "Sadr City, Long a Slum, Now Recovering," *International Herald Tribune*, February 10, 2007.

[98] "District by District, Shiites Make Baghdad Their Own," *New York Times*, December 23, 2006.

[99] Michael E. O'Hanlon, "Break Up Iraq to Save It," *Los Angeles Times*, August 27, 2006.

[100] Michael Abramowitz, "Bush to Press Iraqi Premier on Security," *Washington Post*, November 29, 2006.

trolled neighborhoods with mini-bases, barriers, checkpoints, and identity cards. Having failed to crush the resistance from the top down, the U.S. strategy was now to cut the people off from the insurgents. This model was based on the "new villages" built in Malaysia by the British and the "strategic hamlets" tried by the Americans in Vietnam.[101]

In a hint of things to come, Bush declared that American forces would have a "green light" to enter restive neighborhoods and that "restrictions" on policing would be removed.[102] Bush's military offensive called for at least 4,000 more troops to fight the insurgency in al-Anbar, which he now described as an "al-Qaeda enclave," and more than 17,500 more troops to seize control of neighborhoods in Baghdad.[103]

The basis of sectarian killings has been rationalized by U.S. officials through a document known as the "al-Zarqawi letter," supposedly found on a computer disk on the body of an al-Qaeda-linked courier. Released by the U.S. on February 8, 2004, the letter, which was allegedly signed by Abu Musab al-Zarqawi and written to al-Qaeda, called for provoking a religious civil war in which a Sunni vanguard, led by al-Zarqawi, would attack Shi'a civilians and institutions in order to inflame the Shi'a masses. U.S. officials pointed to the letter as justification of the war on terror, and began blaming casualties on Islamic militants trying to sabotage Western-style democracy. The New York Times military reporter John Burns acknowledged that "questions remain about the letter, including whether the writer really was [al-Zarqawi]." The Times' reporter didn't elaborate on what the "questions" were, but noted that the letter "provided the

---

[101] Julian E. Barnes, "'Gated Communities' Planned for Baghdad," Los Angeles Times, January 11, 2007.
[102] Transcript, "'The Most Urgent Priority for Success in Iraq Is Security,' Bush Says," New York Times, January 11, 2007.
[103] Transcript, New York Times, January 11, 2007.

Americans with a ready-made template for their new inter-pretation of the war."[104]

The al-Zarqawi letter, and the role it played in Iraq's evolving civil war, deserves more scrutiny than it has received. After all, the war itself was partially justified on the basis of forged documents alleging that Saddam sought yellowcake uranium from Niger.

Interested in that case, I traveled in late 2005 to Amman, Jordan, where I interviewed the Iraqi alleged to have been Saddam's agent in seeking yellowcake. His name is Wissam al-Zahawie, and he was serving as the secretary-general of a think tank called the Arab Thought Forum (ATF). Al-Zahawie seemed well-integrated in Jordan; he was at the center of a discussion I had, for example, with Jordan's Prince Hassan. One of the forgeries concerning Niger appeared when al-Zahawie, a career diplomat whose service preceded the reign of Saddam Hussein, was serving at the Vatican. He went to Niger in 1999 at Saddam's request, he said, to offer invitations to several West African countries to visit Baghdad.

"I did not know Niger produced uranium," he told me. He presented officials in Niger the gift of a camel saddle. On Feb-ruary 10, 2003, the Iraqi Foreign Ministry brought him back "urgently" to Baghdad to be interrogated by UN weapons in-spectors. They talked to him for ninety minutes, then called him back for a second meeting where they asked whether he had signed a letter to Niger concerning uranium. He denied signing any such letter and suggested it was a forgery, which turned out to be true. The document was fabricated in Italy, perhaps by someone connected to the Italian intelligence services or to then–Prime Minister Silvio Berlusconi's circle, which might explain why the Vatican-based al-Zahawie's

---

[104] John F. Burns, "Act of Hatred, Hints of Doubt," *New York Times*, April 1, 2004.

name was used. At least one source suggests that the Italian secret services were doing a favor for the U.S.[105]

The whole plot unraveled after the CIA sent former Ambassador Joseph Wilson to investigate the case. When Wilson rejected the Niger yellowcake conspiracy in a *New York Times* op-ed on July 6, 2003, he became the focus of a behind-the-scenes White House smear campaign against him and his wife, Valerie Plame, then a covert CIA operative. The presidency itself was soon threatened, not from the left but from within the CIA. Lost in the scandal was the question of who actually forged the letters and who had knowledge of them, questions al-Zahawie continues to ask.

Forgeries are a staple of U.S. counterintelligence programs. According to a military historian of the Vietnam War, they were a "standard form of statecraft."[106] The CIA's "master forgers could replicate anything," which would then be "inserted into enemy channels" by reconnaissance teams who "would plant the items on an enemy casualty, or in one of its command, logistics, or other NVA facilities on the trail." Among the purposes of these "blackmail operations" were to provoke suspicions and divisions among Vietnamese, and between North Vietnam and China. Thus, it is not paranoid conjecture to ask questions regarding the origins of the 2004 al-Zarqawi letter.

Pentagon estimates for casualties of sectarian violence were

[105] According to a sympathetic history of the Israeli Mossad, an Italian informant alleged that the forged documents were created by Italian intelligence for the CIA and M16 "to support the claim of Blair and Bush that Saddam Hussein had obtained the ore." Who had asked the favor in this case was unknown, "but Mossad knew that in the past the Italian service had bugged the country's presidential palace and the papal library as favor to the CIA"; in Gordon Thomas, *Gideon's Spies: The Secret History of the Mossad* (Thomas Dunne, 2007), pp. 464–5.

[106] Richard H. Shultz, Jr., *The Secret War Against Hanoi: The Untold Story of Spies, Saboteurs, and Covert Warriors in North Vietnam* (HarperCollins, 1999), p. 136.

below 5,000 for the month of January 2006. Then, on February 22, persons unknown blew up al-Askariya Mosque, a sacred Shi'a shrine in Samarra. The ancient site is said by adherents of the largest Shi'a sect to be the 878 A.D. hiding place of the twelfth Imam, Mohammad al-Mahdi. The bombing was a sophisticated operation which required breaching tight security and the remote detonation of a significant explosive charge under the dome. Though credit was claimed by an unknown group, rumors immediately spread that the perpetrators were al-Qaeda members, in keeping with the belief that Sunni terrorists sought to ignite a sectarian war. U.S. authorities immediately blamed al-Qaeda for implementing the plan envisioned in al-Zarqawi's letter, though no evidence was presented.[107] The Shi'a leader Muqtada al-Sadr charged that it was the Americans, not the Sunnis, who were behind the bombing.[108]

Several Iraqi eyewitnesses said that men dressed in military uniforms entered the shrine the previous night, then departed the following morning before the explosion.[109] They somehow overwhelmed a nine-man security force without firing a shot, also escaping the notice of ten other Iraqi officers in the vicinity.[110] Four months later, in June 2006, Iraqi forces arrested and sentenced to death a Tunisian, Yousri Fakher Mohammed Ali, who they claimed had confessed to an al-Qaeda connection during interrogation.[111] He named as the

[107] Peter Galbraith offers an unquestioning explanation of the events in the opening of his book, *The End of Iraq: How American Incompetence Created a War without End* (Simon & Shuster, 2006). "Almost certainly," he says without evidence, "the shrine was destroyed by al-Qaeda."
[108] Robert F. Worth, "Blast Destroys Shrine in Iraq, Setting Off Sectarian Fury," *New York Times*, February 22, 2006.
[109] Personal correspondence with Dal LaMagna, Iraqi Voices Project (Progressive Government Institute), Washington, D.C. LaMagna's sources were eyewitness accounts from Iraqis.
[110] Louise Roug, "The Day Civil War Erupted in Iraq," *Los Angeles Times*, February 13, 2007.
[111] "The Day Civil War Erupted in Iraq," *Los Angeles Times*, February 13, 2007.

mastermind a Sunni, Haytham al-Badri, who has never been apprehended.[112]

There was no holding back popular Shi'a rage, however. This was like blowing up the Vatican. Retaliatory attacks were inflicted on 184 Sunni mosques. One thousand people were killed in just a few days, as civil war began in earnest.[113] The Pentagon reported a tremendous increase in Iraqi casualties, reaching 120 per day by the summer.[114] Despite the lack of any evidence, the Samarra bombing became the key to the Bush Administration's official narrative of how al-Qaeda provoked the Shi'a to retaliate with death squads supported by Iran. "And the result was a vicious cycle of sectarian violence that continues today," Bush told Americans in his televised address of January 2007 to promote his "new way forward" strategy in Iraq.[115]

It may only be another coincidence, but prior to the Samarra bombing, top U.S. military commanders like General George Casey were preparing proposals to begin withdrawing tens of thousands of American troops. "U.S. Starts Laying Groundwork for Significant Troop Pullout from Iraq" declared a Los Angeles Times dispatch from Washington.[116] A London Times headline in early 2006 also announced that "Allies Signal Big Pullout from Iraq."[117] The Iraqi cochair of a joint U.S.–Iraqi security committee, soon to be a national security adviser, was

---

[112] "The Day Civil War Erupted in Iraq," Los Angeles Times, February 13, 2007. See also, Marc Santora, "One Year Later, Golden Mosque Is Still in Ruins," New York Times, February 11, 2007.

[113] Galbraith, p. 2.

[114] Michael R. Gordon, "Iraqi Casualties Are Up Sharply, U.S. Study Finds," New York Times, September 2, 2006.

[115] Transcript, "President's Address to the Nation," White House (Office of the Press Secretary, January 10, 2007). Of course, the Shi'a death squads (or militias) were formed years before the Samarra bombing.

[116] Paul Richter and Tyler Marshall, "U.S. Starts Laying Groundwork for Significant Troop Pullout from Iraq," Los Angeles Times, November 26, 2005.

[117] Richard Beeston and Daniel McGrory, "Allies Signal Big Pullout from Iraq," Times (U.K.), February 2, 2006.

even more specific, saying that foreign troop levels would fall from 160,000 to less than 100,000 in 2006, and that "by the end of 2007 the overwhelming majority of the multinational forces will have left the country."[118] Instruction books were already prepared, the Iraqi official said, identifying the order of departure of the units.

Then came the explosions at Samarra.

Largely ruled out was any discussion of the possibility that the conspirators were unknown provocateurs.[119] Even if Western special operations forces had nothing to do with Samarra, it was a moment to acknowledge their long history of dirty tricks, fabricated incidents, propaganda, psychological warfare, and fanning of factional rivalries.[120] The U.S. was ex-

---

[118] "Allies Signal Big Pullout from Iraq," *Times* (U.K.), February 2, 2006.

[119] As noted, the CIA paid the Iraqi National Accord to launch car bomb attacks and assassinations against Ba'athists in an effort to overthrow Saddam, under the leadership of Iyad Allawi, who became the U.S.-appointed prime minister. In McGovern and Polk, p. 48.

[120] Though little known to the American people, the U.S. and British have long histories of such "counterintelligence" operations, described as the "wilderness of mirrors" by the CIA chief of counterintelligence, James Angleton. The U.S. paid for and staged "riots" to overthrow the nationalist government of Iran in 1953; the British sent out undercover operatives to shoot pro-Republican lawyers and intentionally provoked inter-communal violence. During the Vietnam War, the CIA directed Operation Phoenix, aimed at eliminating the Vietcong infrastructure by killing alleged VC agents. Toward North Vietnam, the U.S. counterinsurgency programs included the complete fabrication of an underground resistance movement, the Sacred Sword of the Patriots League, and used the agency's "master-forgers" to plant letters and documents meant to divide Hanoi from China. The CIA's counterintelligence organization was touted as a "mighty Wurlitzer" capable of playing many tunes, all designed to "drive them crazy with psywar." For sources of this history, see Richard Shultz, formerly of the Naval War College, *The Secret War Against Hanoi* (HarperCollins, 1999). For British operations in Northern Ireland, see Nicholas Davies, *Ten Thirty-Three: The Inside Story of Britain's Secret Killing Machine in Northern Ireland* (Mainstream Publishing, 1999). The author writes that "most senior government ministers in the Northern Ireland Office in London believed that if the Provos [the Provisional Irish Republican Army] could be defeated then the loyalist groups, including the UDA [a loyalist militia], would end their own military campaign and peace would return to Northern Ireland" (p. 146). Applied to Iraq, this thinking would justify eliminating the Sunni insurgency so that the Shi'a militias would put down their arms. Davies, a unionist admirer,

posed as operating a secret "black room" at Camp Nama, part of a shadowy warrior unit known as Task Force 6-26, where the slogan was "No blood, no foul," as they tried extracting information on al-Zarqawi.[121] In a 2005 online article suggestively titled "The Salvador Option," *Newsweek* reported that "the Pentagon may put Special Forces–led assassination or kidnapping teams in Iraq."[122]

An analysis of a special tally conducted during the December 2005 parliamentary elections suggested that only seven percent of the Iraqi army was Sunni.[123] That year, Bayan Jabr, leader of SCIRI's Badr Brigade, took over the Interior Ministry and filled it with Shi'a commandos who dragged Sunnis from their homes, shot them in their heads, and poured acid on their faces.[124] The ministry operated as many as ten unofficial jails in Baghdad, run by special interrogation units who reported only to the Badr Brigade.[125] The State Department itself commented on the security bodies, describing how they engaged in "threats, intimidation, beatings, and suspension by the arms or legs, as well as the reported use of electrical drills and cords and the application of electric shocks."[126]

The report also noted the November 2005 discovery and forced closure of a detention center with 169 Sunni captives,

documented a secret plan to provide photographs, names, addresses, and car registration numbers to loyalist death squads. To maximize fear, the targets of the killings included not only IRA guerrillas but "Sinn Féin politicians, Republican sympathizers, and, unbelievably, decent, ordinary Catholics" (p. 65).

[121] Eric Schmitt and Carolyn Marshall, "In Secret Unit's 'Black Room,' a Grim Portrait of U.S. Abuse," *New York Times*, March 19, 2006.

[122] Michael Hirsh and John Barry, "The Salvador Option," *Newsweek*, January 8, 2005 (http://www.msnbc.msn.com/id/6802629/site/newsweek/).

[123] Richard A. Oppel Jr., "Iraq Vote Shows Sunnis Are Few in Military," *New York Times*, December 27, 2005.

[124] Dexter Filkins, "Sunnis Accuse Iraqi Military of Kidnappings and Slayings," *New York Times*, November 29, 2005.

[125] Edward Wong and John F. Burns, "Iraqi Rift Grows As Secret Prison Enrages Sunnis," *New York Times*, November 17, 2005.

[126] Brian Knowlton, "Iraqi Police Are Tied to Abuses and Deaths, U.S. Report Finds," *New York Times*, March 9, 2006.

"many of whom showed signs of torture," and the uncovering in December of a police building with 625 prisoners "in conditions so crowded that detainees were unable to lie down at the same time," several of whom showed "severe signs of torture."[127]

A retired army colonel named James Steele helped develop the Iraqi police units, and as of 2006, Major General Joseph Peterson was leading their training. Ann Bertucci, an American with the "civilian police assistance training team," has acknowledged that U.S. advisers were attached to the Iraqi brigade that massacred thirty-six Sunnis in one night, but denied allegations of their direct involvement.[128] The U.S. military also said in 2006 that it only "recently learned" that the 7,700-member public order brigades, expanded when the Badr Brigade took over the Interior Ministry in 2005, were virtually all Shi'a.[129] A Committee for the Missing was formed in Kirkuk in 2006 to search for 100 "disappeared" people, mostly Sunnis, who were "believed to have been arrested by Kurdish and U.S. forces."[130] Colonel Steele, speaking of the special police in 2006, told the New York Times that he did "not regret their creation," but that the U.S. had lost control.[131]

In 2005, armed British special agents were caught disguised as Arab militants in Basra, with no explanation being offered for their undercover operation. Later, London's Sunday Telegraph reported that Britain was recruiting Iraqi

[127] "Iraqi Police Are Tied to Abuses and Deaths, U.S. Report Finds," New York Times, March 9, 2006.
[128] Michael Moss, "How Iraq Police Reform Became Casualty of War," New York Times, May 22, 2006.
[129] Edward Wong, "U.S. Is Seeking Better Balance in Iraqi Police," New York Times, March 7, 2006.
[130] Solomon Moore, "Tensions Simmer As Kurds Reclaim Kirkuk," Los Angeles Times, May 12, 2006.
[131] "How Iraq Police Reform Became Casualty of War," New York Times, May 22, 2006.

double agents for operations coordinated from a secret "joint support group" inside the Green Zone.[132] Such occasional windows into this shadow world reveal nothing concrete about agent provocateurs or counterintelligence, but are fragments of what Vice President Cheney anticipated shortly after September 11:

> We also have to work . . . sort of on the dark side, if you will. We've got to spend time in the shadows of the intelligence world. A lot of what needs to be done here will have to be done quietly, without any discussion.[133]

This is not to say that the Bush Administration *planned* on civil war; evidence supports the view that it did not. Many neoconservatives like William Kristol were convinced that the different Iraqi ethnic and religous groups could get along in a U.S.-liberated Iraq; most Shi'a, for example, fought alongside Sunnis in the long war against Iran. But the nature of the occupation itself forced open past sectarian wounds. The U.S. installed the Shi'a in power, not a secular government. The U.S. armed and tolerated the infiltration of pro-Iran Shi'a militias into Iraqi security forces, then let them carry on the "Salvadoran option" and who yet knows what else. The U.S. introduced a political process in which every Iraqi was classified as Shi'a, Sunni, Turkmen, etc., for purposes of representation. Where Saddam's dictatorship kept a lid on ethnic divisions while delivering educational and economic benefits to the Iraqi middle class, the U.S. invasion caused sectarian conflict to explode and the professional class to leave the

---

[132] Sean Rayment, "Top Secret Army Cell Breaks Terrorists," *Sunday Telegraph*, February 5, 2007.
[133] Cited in Joseph Lelyveld, "Interrogating Ourselves," *New York Times Magazine*, June 12, 2005, p. 39.

country. Two million people have left Iraq since the invasion; an additional 1.9 million are listed as "internally displaced," including 727,000 since the 2006 Samarra bombing.[134]

The Insurgency's Lack of Political Voice

The insurgency is often described as lacking a political arm or party. Rough comparisons are sometimes made to Sinn Féin in Northern Ireland or the National Front for the Liberation of South Vietnam (NLF). But the absence of a close parallel to Iraq is seen as further evidence that the insurgency is incoherent and leaderless—a fragmented rebellion with which negotiations are impossible.

Is this analysis accurate, and if not, what political platform does the resistance have?

First of all, neither Sinn Féin nor the NLF were welcomed to the table by their respective occupying powers—Britain and the United States. Both were criminalized, forced to function in semi-clandestine conditions, penetrated by spies and provocateurs, and constantly subjected to offers that would co-opt and divide them.

It is true that the Iraqi resistance is more divided internally than were the Irish Republicans and Vietnamese revolutionaries. Time, however, blurs the divisions that the U.K. promoted, for example, between Irish Republicans and "constitutional nationalists," and between Catholics and Protestants in Northern Ireland; and that the U.S. promoted between the NLF and tribal people like the Montagnards, or between the NLF and Buddhists in South Vietnam.

Besides the major differences between Sunnis and Shi'a

---

[134] Kristèle Younès, "The World's Fastest Growing Displacement Crisis: Displaced People inside Iraq Receiving Inadequate Assistance," Refugees International, March 2007.

over post-Saddam Iraq, another key reason for the lack of a unified platform or party is the threat of violence and assassination. Most public figures in Iraq, whether Sunni or Shi'a, are vulnerable to violent assault. The Sunni peace parliamentarian Saleh al-Mutlaq was nearly killed after attempting to change the Iraqi regime from within. And in mid-April 2007, an attack on the Iraqi Parliament within the heavily fortified Green Zone killed Muhammad Awad, a Sunni legislator from al-Mutlaq's National Dialogue Front, plunging the government into further chaos.[135] The lack of meaningful security is a major deterrent to the emergence of political leaders from within the resistance.

Nevertheless, it is far from true that the insurgency is an unreachable, anonymous network of hit squads. Since 2003, there have been numerous occasions of contact and dialogue between insurgent leaders, political or clerical intermediaries, and responsible American commanders and embassy personnel. In December 2003, a UN staff member delivered the message to the U.S. embassy that the insurgents were "keen to open a dialogue with the coalition, through the UN."[136] An American official, Larry Diamond, sent a memo to Condoleezza Rice arguing that if the Sunni insurgents were given a meaningful role in the new Iraq, "they may be persuaded to give up violence as an option, *and Iraqi and coalition casualties may decline, saving many lives in the coming months.*"[137]

The failure of numerous contacts to produce cease-fires or peace plans is not only due to Iraqi factionalism, but also to the expectation that insurgents should immediately surrender,

---

[135] Edward Wong, "Qaeda Group in Iraq Says It Led Attack on Parliament," *New York Times*, April 14, 2007.
[136] Larry Diamond, *Squandered Victory* (Owl Books/Henry Holt, 2006), p. 64.
[137] Diamond, p. 65. Italics in original.

then take their chances.[138] But the insurgents want assurances that the U.S. intends to withdraw before they consider cease-fires and the beginning of a political settlement.

My direct experience with this process began in 2005 when I became frustrated with the lack of media recognition that the Iraqi insurgents might have actual political aspirations. I sought out Iraqi resistance supporters in London in 2005, then traveled to Amman, Jordan to meet with Iraqi exiles twice in 2006.

On my first visit, with Ted Lewis of the peace group Global Exchange, I stayed at the home of a former Jordanian minister introduced to me by a member of the U.S. Congress, Jim Mc-Dermott of Washington State. I was asked to speak to members of the Arab Thought Forum, and to attend a social gathering with numerous Iraqi exiles, including former ministers and technicians from Saddam's government. I drove through neighborhoods overflowing with Iraqis displaced by the war.

One morning, Ted and I were visited by an Iraqi (and his driver) who had traveled fifteen hours from Baghdad to brief us on the resistance. For security reasons, I cannot provide his name, but he seemed to be a genuine intermediary, fluent in English, with contacts to the insurgency. He lived in a Baghdad neighborhood where Sunnis, Shi'a, Kurds, and Christians commingled before the 2003 invasion.

While many Iraqis fundamentally believed that battling American forces was the only way to be taken seriously, some also felt it necessary to offer their own ideas for a lasting settlement. I found their proposals interesting and reasonable,

---

[138] As a typical example, a *New York Times* headline on January 7, 2006 read, "Americans Said to Meet Rebels, Exploiting Rift." The talks were aimed at urging the Sunni insurgency to fight against al-Qaeda. The process broke down, said a Sunni intermediary, over the "demand by the insurgents for a timetable for withdrawal of American troops, which President Bush has repeatedly refused" (Dexter Filkins and Sabrina Tavernise).

though they clearly derived from Sunni and Ba'athist perspectives.[139] This Iraqi stressed that these proposals were designed to respect "the interests of the United States as a superpower"; further, he assured us that American corporations would be allowed to bid competitively on postwar contracts, and that Iraq had no plans to "drink our oil" but wanted to sell it on world markets. With respect to resolving the military conflict, he passed on these recommendations:

• immediate inclusion of more opposition voices, like the Association of Muslim Scholars and the newly formed National Dialogue Council, in the ongoing discussion of how to achieve a balanced constitution. These could implicitly represent the resistance;

• an announced timetable for American troop withdrawals, as also voiced at the Cairo conference sponsored by the Arab League in November 2006;

• acceptance of the legitimacy of "national resistance," also endorsed by the Arab League (as opposed to the jihadist path of al-Qaeda);

• establishment of a new caretaker government in Baghdad, including the opposition alongside the ruling Shi'a and Kurdish parties;

• a fixed deadline for new, inclusive elections;

• a peacekeeping force, endorsed by the United Na-

[139] Full interview, "Pacifying Iraq: Insurgent Scenarios," available from the *Nation* website, January 10, 2006 (http://www.thenation.com/doc/20060123/hayden).

tions, composed of countries "not involved in the occupation." (He specifically mentioned France, Germany, Switzerland, Austria, Indonesia, Malaysia, Pakistan, Egypt, Algeria, Sudan, Yemen, and Morocco);

• renewed reconstruction assistance, including contracts for American firms;

• removal of high-ranking Ba'athists, but not at the expense of destroying the Iraqi national state. The new government would determine whom to punish and whom to restore from the former regime.

Later that week we were driven to Prince Hassan's grounds for a discussion with him and his circle of advisers. The prince passionately promoted a win-win settlement, guaranteeing oil for the West alongside real Sunni representation in Iraqi governance. Recent bombings of four Amman hotels by unknown militants underscored the urgency of his statements. As we left, after two hours of discussion, Prince Hassan stood in his driveway, smiling and waving goodbye. Realizing that the war was already spilling over the kingdom's borders, I momentarily visualized Iraq emptied of Sunnis altogether, their survivors melting into the surroundings of Jordan, just as the Palestinians arrived there some forty years before.

I traveled once again to Jordan in 2006 for an unprecedented peace meeting organized by Global Exchange, CODEPINK, and their Iraqi contacts. Reflecting the significance of the event, the Iraqis sent representatives from each of their blocs in Parliament, Shi'a and Sunni, as well as other parliamentarians, members of the Association of Muslim Scholars, and victims of torture at

Abu Ghraib. The all-day sessions took place over a long weekend at the modest Toledo Hotel in Amman. Nearly twenty Americans attended, almost all from peace and justice groups, several with military or diplomatic backgrounds.

Some of the Iraqi parliamentarians present had tenuous relations to the various militias, and perhaps only an indirect understanding of the insurgents' agenda. They were knowledgeable intermediaries, not representatives authorized to negotiate. But it was clear as the discussions progressed that there existed a tentative goal shared by both Sunni and Shi'a: The U.S. should set a deadline for withdrawal, and during the same time frame make efforts to repair the problems created by the occupation. These problems included uncontrolled militias and the distribution of oil revenues, among others.

The point being made was that the insurgency would only decline, whether organically or by local negotiation, when the U.S. makes a sincere decision to withdraw militarily from Iraq. It was also evident that any deadline for withdrawal would have to be flexible. "Out now" had been bypassed by recent events. Most of these Iraqis were caught between the demands of their constituents for withdrawal, the pressures of death squads on those same constituencies, and their relationships with the Americans protecting their privileged status in the Green Zone. While there was a consensus that the American troops should go home, there was also a desire by some for them to stay, at least temporarily, for protection.

The divide-and-conquer policies were working, as the same Iraqis who two years before had called for immediate and unconditional withdrawal were now worrying whether such a move would place them at risk. The new formula called for two deadlines: one for withdrawal, another for fixing the problems that American policies had created. In March 2007, a European–U.S. poll of Iraqis revealed that thirty-five percent thought the U.S. should "leave now," while seventy-eight percent opposed the occupation and sixty-nine percent felt the U.S. presence was destabilizing security.[140]

The key Iraqi player at the Amman meeting appeared to be Saleh al-Mutlaq, a Sunni parliamentarian heading a bloc known as the Iraqi Front for National Dialogue. An ex-Ba'athist and Sunni, al-Mutlaq dressed in a conservative gray suit, chain-smoked, and spoke evenly, clearly, but urgently. During the 2005 national election, he noted, 100 election workers for his own party had been killed. The party's resulting eleven seats were a disappointment, but by allying with other parties, including Shi'a nationalists, al-Mutlaq might achieve his goal of a coalition demanding a U.S. withdrawal. "There should be a timetable for withdrawing troops plus a parallel timetable for fixing their mistakes," he said. By fixing mistakes, he meant the overwhelming tasks of dismantling death squads, reversing the blanket de-Ba'athification orders, executing a reconciliation plan, and committing to continued postwar reconstruction. It was painful for him, but al-Mutlaq was accepting the practical realities of the occupation, in which U.S. troops were sometimes the only protectors of Sunni communities; while at the same time, he wanted the occupation to end. He explained:

> *The Arab Sunnis were the most anti–U.S. occupation, but now the U.S. is trying to take advantage of their vulnerability and wants them to ask the U.S. to stay . . . The death squads are to implement the "new Middle East project"* [of the neoconservatives] *. . . It is based on making our countries smaller and dividing people. Federalism is*

[140] Poll conducted by D3 Systems for BBC, ABC News, German ARD TV, and *USA Today*, February 25–March 5, 2007.

the start of partition and civil war, starting ethnic conflicts
over borders and oil.

I learned that al-Mutlaq had a plan for a kind of peaceful coup against the American-supported al-Maliki regime.
The notion came from a chance meeting with an American
contractor in Baghdad, a retired marine with close ties to the
Sunnis. In documents dated November 13 and 16, 2006, the
blueprint included:

- immediate meetings between the Sunni insurgent
groups and top American generals toward a cease-fire;
- a proposal for an interim government chosen by
Parliament to replace the al-Maliki regime;
- restoration and re-integration of underground ex-
Ba'athist military units into the national structure;
- greater efforts by the U.S.-led multinational force
(MNF-I) aimed at controlling militias and securing
the border with Iran;
- a status-of-forces agreement permitting the presence of U.S. troops for a decade, but with reductions
and redeployments phased over time;
- negotiated amnesty and prisoner releases, with
Americans guaranteeing the prohibitions on torture
in Shi'a-controlled state detention centers;
- rescinding of Paul Bremer's de-Ba'athification edicts;
- continued American financing of reconstruction
along with war-debt relief for Kuwait.

Whether drafted by Iraqis or Americans, or both, this was
a plan to de-escalate the war without appearing to force an
abrupt American troop withdrawal. The key was replacing

the al-Maliki circle with a nonsectarian transitional government until new elections could be called. This strategy could
work if it was acceptable to al-Sadr's Shi'a bloc of parliamentarians plus a few independents from smaller parties. I learned
from an Iraqi analyst in London that support for a one-year
withdrawal existed among 140 to 160 Iraqi parliamentarians,
enough for ratification.

The opportunity for the coup suddenly arose when al-
Sadr's party boycotted Parliament in objection to al-Maliki's
meeting with Bush in Amman in late 2006. For a brief moment, it seemed possible that the parliamentarians could bring
down al-Maliki. Al-Mutlaq certainly hoped for this outcome.
CNN was the only media outlet covering what was called a
"possible new political alliance" on November 30.[141] They
interviewed al-Mutlaq, who called the bloc a "nonsectarian
national patriotic front." He said that al-Sadr was "not negative" about the alliance, which could be achieved through
peaceful means.

Then, suddenly, the scheme fizzled, for reasons still unknown. Perhaps it was a Sunni fantasy that al-Sadr would
join. Or perhaps the U.S. intervened to suppress the threat.

Al-Mutlaq paid a steep price. On January 1, 2007, American and Iraqi forces stormed his Baghdad house, killing six
people, including a family of four. The reason given was an
unsubstantiated rumor that the place was an al-Qaeda "safe-
house."[142] It seemed preposterous to me. In a telephone interview with an Iraqi based in Washington, al-Mutlaq's assistant
described the victims as two security guards and a family with
small children. The more likely explanation for the attack

[141] "Al-Sadr Bloc Talks of Alliance with Sunnis, Christians," CNN, November
30, 2006.
[142] "Angry Protests in Iraq Suggest Sunni Arab Shift to Militants," *New York
Times*, January 2, 2007.

was someone's payback for al-Mutlaq's ongoing effort to put a peace coalition in power.

Even the peace parliamentarians were targets. Who would step forward again?

But it was not over for al-Mutlaq. If the military conflict was locked in a stalemate, the only solution would be political. If the executives of the two nations were frozen in a failed project, the parliamentarians and social movements would have to act. As a result of the "citizen's diplomacy" between Americans and Iraqis, there finally came the first dialogue between members of the Iraqi Parliament and the U.S. Congress, on March 8, 2007. The unprecedented two-hour dialogue took place via teleconference from a congressional recording studio in the Rayburn House Office Building in Washington, with nine elected officials from the U.S. and six from Iraq. The Americans were led by Representative Jim McDermott, the Iraqis by the irrepressible al-Mutlaq and al-Jabiri of al-Fadhila. This teleconference might have been the first official bilateral step in an earnest effort to promote peace.[143]

THE BLIND SPOT IN AMERICAN COUNTERINSURGENCY

Not only had the U.S. failed to increase its intelligence-gathering capacity toward the resistance, but by late 2006,

---

[143] The teleconference on March 8, 2007 included Democrats Jim McDermott, William Delahunt, Keith Ellison, Jay Inslee, Lynne Woolsey, and Mike Honda, and Republicans Christopher Shays, Wayne Gilchrest, and Thomas Petri. The Iraqis were al-Mutlaq, al-Jabiri, Hassan al-Shammari of al-Fadhila, Mohammed al-Dynee of the National Dialogue Front, Sheik Khalaf al-Elayyan of the Sunni National Dialogue Council, and Osama al-Nujaifi of Iyad Allawi's secular Iraqi National List. It was facilitated and translated by Raed Jarrar, a young Iraqi who performed the same duties at the earlier Amman dialogue, and by Dal LaMagna of the Iraqi Voices Project. Transcripts from the meeting are available courtesy of the Iraqi Voices Project (Progressive Government Institute), Washington, D.C. (http://progressivegovernment. org/page.php?name=March8Transcript).

the army was only just beginning to shift its official doctrine to confront "irregular warfare." This development was aided by university anthropologists who fantasized that counter-insurgency was "armed social science."[144] The new army and marine doctrines of counterinsurgency were made available as drafts in October 2006, and would be refined by General David Petraeus. They described "representative paradoxes" such as:

- *The more you protect your force, the less secure you are. If military forces stay locked up in compounds, they lose touch with the people, appear to be running scared, and cede the initiative to the insurgents.*
- *Tactical success guarantees nothing.*
- *If a tactic works this week, it might not work next week; if it works in this province, it might not work in the next.*[145]

One can only imagine young, scared, trigger-happy American troops reading over these little axioms before heading into a town where everyone looks unfamiliar and speaks another language, in a country where the average age is less than twenty years and many people favor attacks on American soldiers.

Considering these dilemmas, an expert at a Washington think tank asked of U.S. policy makers, "What would Pepsi-Cola or Disney do?" in an interview with the *New Yorker* correspondent George Packer.[146] The very question reveals the state of denial that plagues U.S. efforts to address the insur-

[144] The phrase is from a former captain in the Australian army, David Kilcullen, whose writings on counterinsurgency are widely studied in the U.S. military. See George Packer, "Knowing the Enemy," *New Yorker*, December 18, 2006.
[145] Michael R. Gordon, "Military Hones a New Strategy on Insurgency," *New York Times*, October 5, 2006.
[146] "Knowing the Enemy," *New Yorker*, December 18, 2006.

gency. It took three years of denying that there could even be an insurgency, followed by a public relations rationalization of the occupation. The problem, from Packer's viewpoint, is that the rapid proliferation of information through new technology makes counterinsurgency more difficult because it depends on secrecy—public disclosure of techniques like torture makes too many Americans uncomfortable. A similar view is held by leading neoconservative Robert Kaplan, who called for "Supremacy by Stealth" in the July/August 2003 issue of the *Atlantic Monthly*. Kaplan, who often travels with U.S. Special Forces, counsels that "the best information strategy is to avoid attention-getting confrontations in the first place and to keep the public's attention as divided as possible. We can dominate the world only quietly: off camera, so to speak."

Such an approach calls for stealth at all times, an inconvenience given freedom of the press. But the alternative to secret wars, Kaplan says, is a serious threat—the emergence of antiwar movements:

> *The moment the public focuses on a single crisis like the one in Iraq, that crisis is no longer analyzed on its merits: Instead it becomes a rallying point around which lonely and alienated people in a global mass society can define themselves through an uplifting group identity, be it European, Muslim, antiwar intellectual, or whatever.*

Keeping Secrets, Threatening Democracy

Every effort is made to keep the Iraq War "off camera, so to speak." The relentless air strikes that have continued since the invasion are virtually unknown, rarely mentioned in the

Washington Post, the *New York Times*, or *Time* magazine during 2005, according to one researcher.[147] Yet during November 2005 alone, the air force launched 996 bombing sorties and, during the month-long siege of Fallujah a year earlier, twenty-six tons of bombs were dropped by the navy and marines.[148] But this secrecy was nothing in comparison to the cover-ups of casualty rates on all sides.

The number of reported American casualties was obscured by the official ban on photographs of coffins returning to an air base outside of Washington, until a freedom-of-information lawsuit forced the release of a photo of somber honor guards carrying the flag-draped remains of their comrades.[149] The Pentagon tries to limit U.S. casualty figures to those killed in *actual* combat, as if accidental deaths are not wartime casualties. Even in 2007, tens of thousands of wounded American soldiers were still being deleted from the official count.[150] Then there were questions of whether badly wounded Americans who died on their way to hospitals in Europe, and therefore outside of Iraqi airspace, should be counted in the official death toll. American contractors who died on the battlefield were not included in the official casualty rates either; at least 770 deaths in the privatized security forces were estimated by the end of 2006.[151]

---

[147] Norman Solomon, "Hidden in Plane Sight: U.S. Media Dodging Air War in Iraq," Fairness and Accuracy in Reporting, *Media Beat*, December 6, 2005.

[148] Dahr Jamail, "An Increasingly Aerial Occupation," Tomdispatch.com, December 13, 2005 (http://www.tomdispatch.com/index.mhtml?pid=42286).

[149] Bill Carter, "Pentagon Ban on Pictures of Dead Troops Is Broken," *New York Times*, April 23, 2004.

[150] Denise Grady, "Agency Says Higher Casualty Total Was Posted in Error," *New York Times*, January 30, 2007. Including all U.S. wounded in Iraq and Afghanistan, the real number is 50,508. But by deleting noncombat and "nonhostile" injuries, the number drops to 21,649. Of 1.4 million Americans who have served in Iraq and Afghanistan, 205,000 have sought assistance from the veterans' agency.

[151] Jeremy Scahill, "Bush's Shadow Army," *Nation*, April 2, 2007.

Equally shocking is the deliberate American attempt to minimize Iraqi casualty rates since 2003. At first the U.S. denied keeping such records at all. "We don't do body counts," said General Tommy Franks.[152] By April 2007, an organization called the Iraq Body Count estimated between 60,000 and 65,000 Iraqi deaths, based on combing through media sources—a technique with severe limits. Some reporters sought information from local morgues, or from the Iraqi health ministry, which processes death certificates. These were also unreliable, since many of the dead were scattered in fields and ditches, or buried immediately in the ground as per Muslim custom. A rigorous study by Johns Hopkins and Iraqi medical researchers based on 1,849 households estimated an excess-mortality rate of 654,965 Iraqis (between 2003 and 2006) above the number that would have been expected (based on the year leading up to the invasion).[153] These staggering numbers were covered as a one-day story by most of the U.S. media, and there was little follow-up. The momentary headlines did little to offset the ingrained assumption that Iraqi deaths were somehow "minimal."

The Iraq Study Group Report cataloged the official techniques of underreporting the violence:

A murder of an Iraqi is not necessarily counted as an attack. If we cannot determine the source of a sectarian attack, that assault does not make it into the database. A roadside bomb or a rocket or a mortar attack that doesn't hurt U.S. personnel doesn't count.

[152] Cited in Edward Epstein, "How Many Iraqis Died? We May Never Know," *San Francisco Chronicle*, May 3, 2003.
[153] "The Human Cost of the War in Iraq, A Mortality Study, 2002–2006," Bloomberg School of Public Health (Johns Hopkins University) and the School of Medicine (al-Mustansiriya University), in cooperation with the Center for International Studies (Massachusetts Institute of Technology).

On a single day the ISG studied, there were ninety-three significant acts of violence officially reported, but a careful review of the data brought to light close to 1,100 acts of violence.[154]

The U.S. government had learned certain lessons of Vietnam very well, especially the management of perceptions, keeping troubling information off camera. The information war must be directed against the American people, lest their sensitivities mobilize them to action.

However, any counterinsurgency which merely attempts to disguise U.S. dominance in the affairs of another people will fail. And a democratic state cannot long survive its own attempts to hide the facts from its people.

From the Wise Men of 1968 to the Iraq Study Group of 2006

A U.S. government mechanism for dealing with a paralyzing crisis, when checks-and-balances break down, is through the intervention of a blue-ribbon elite committee committed to the American system as a whole. In the worst days of the Vietnam War, it was the "Wise Men," a circle of diplomats, retired generals, bankers, and corporate lawyers, who flatly told President Johnson that the costs of the Vietnam War were greater than the benefits, that the time had come to cut U.S. losses before they worsened, in both Asia and domestically. The same purpose may be served by the Baker-Hamilton Iraq Study Group, which issued a warning in December 2006 that the Iraq War may be militarily unwinnable. It was a sharp rebuke to the neoconservative vision.

[154] *The Iraq Study Group Report*, p. 95.

Despite a massive effort, stability in Iraq remains elusive and the situation is deteriorating . . . The ability of the United States to shape outcomes is diminishing. Time is running out . . . U.S. forces seem to be caught in a mission that has no foreseeable end . . . A slide toward chaos could trigger the collapse of Iraq's government and a humanitarian catastrophe . . . Americans could become more polarized.[155]

There is a notable difference between the Wise Men of 1968 and the Baker-Hamilton group of 2006. The former was a cross-section of elite "gentlemen" used to operating in Machiavellian fashion behind the scenes, acting like lawyers providing confidential advice to their client, the president. Its core members—Dean Acheson, Charles Bohlen, Clark Clifford, Abe Fortas, W. Averell Harriman, McGeorge Bundy, Maxwell Taylor, Omar Bradley, Robert Murphy, Henry Cabot Lodge, Arthur H. Dean, C. Douglas Dillon, and George Ball— had earlier been consulted by LBJ on the eve of the 1965 U.S. escalation, which they approved.[156] Four of the eleven had attended Groton School. They fit C. Wright Mills's definition of the *power elite*.

The Baker-Hamilton Iraq Study Group differed in composition. Four were former elected officials, and the group was balanced with five Republicans and five Democrats. Like the Wise Men, they represented a confluence of state, corporate, and military interests. Two of them, James Baker and Lawrence Eagleberger, were past secretaries of state. Lee Hamilton, a longtime congressional leader, was vice-chairman of the 9-11 Commission, which issued its report in 2004. There

[155] *The Iraq Study Group Report*, pp. 32, 12, xiv.
[156] Walter Isaacson and Evan Thomas, *The Wise Men: Six Friends and the World They Made* (Simon & Schuster, 1986), p. 677.

was a former White House chief of staff, two leaders with military backgrounds, and a retired Supreme Court justice.

Unlike the Wise Men, this group included one woman and one African-American man, both Beltway insiders. The group shared common interests in the private sector.[157] Baker is senior partner in Baker Botts, a powerhouse lawfirm representing oil interests in the Middle East. Eagleberger is a former president of Kissinger Associates, board member of Halliburton and Phillips Petroleum, and senior partner in another powerful law firm, Baker, Donelson, Bearman and Caldwell. The Democrat, and Clinton confidant, Vernon Jordan, in addition to having led the National Urban League, is a senior counsel at Akin Gump Strauss Haur and Feld, and involved in the Bilderberg meetings, a secret trilateral conference of American, European, and Japanese corporate heavyweights.

The Baker-Hamilton group also consulted a narrow band of "former officials and experts," apparently none of whom advocated withdrawal from Iraq.[158] Seven of these forty-three experts were U.S. generals, five were secretaries of state, four were national security advisers, and five others were retired public officials. At least seven of the non-officials were known advocates of the 2003 invasion, three of them fervent neoconservatives (William Kristol, Frederick Kagan, and Douglas Feith). The panels and working groups included representatives of Citigroup, Bechtel, the Heritage Foundation, the Rand Corporation, and the Brookings Institution. None of the experts had antiwar, civil rights, health, or environmental backgrounds. It is fair to say this was a more diversified group than the Wise Men, revealing changes in American society,

[157] *The Iraq Study Group Report*, pp. 124–40. This biographical information is from the appendix of the report.
[158] The exception was Mark Danner, whose research and writings on Abu Ghraib have shaped the American debate on torture. See *Torture and Truth: America, Abu Ghraib, and the War on Terror* (New York Review of Books, 2004).

but nevertheless reflected a conservative definition of the country's institutional interests.

Unlike the Wise Men, the Baker-Hamilton Iraq Study Group rushed its report straight to the American public through a huge marketing campaign. It landed in thousands of bookstores across the country at precisely 11 a.m. on December 6, 2006, the moment of its release at an overflowing press conference in Washington, D.C.

The proposals included setting a "goal," an aspiration rather than a timetable, for withdrawing U.S. *combat* brigades by May 2008. While this might markedly reduce American casualties, it would leave tens of thousands of American advisers embedded in a dysfunctional Iraqi army without a deadline for coming home. To avert this danger, the report recommended an extensive blueprint for political inclusion, much along the lines advocated by the Sunnis, but with an emphasis on dialogue with al-Sadr and al-Sistani. There was even an implied threat to end support for the current Iraqi regime if it could not contain sectarian divisions. A further emphasis, sharply diverging from the Bush White House, was a diplomatic offensive including talks with Iran and Syria.

Moderate as they might seem, these Baker-Hamilton proposals represented a fundamental breakup of the consensus that had ruled Washington over the previous six years and a complete rebuke of the neoconservative agenda. The group's intent was to inform and engage the American people, who had voted against the war in the November 7 congressional elections, against the president and the neoconservatives still holding onto power. This was an effort to provide a face-saving retreat for American forces in Iraq, a mirror of the last days in Vietnam. And it was designed to prevent the further polarization of American opinion. Though never openly said, it was also intended to diminish the impact of the antiwar movement on the coming 2008 elections.

The interests of Baker's close associates in the American oil lobby were represented in recommendations 62 and 63 of the report.[159] The first was a suggestion that the U.S. government help draft an Iraqi oil law—a process that was already well underway. Recommendation 63 urged that the U.S. assist in transforming the national oil industry of Iraq into a "commercial enterprise" in order to encourage investment by multinational oil companies. As a matter of philosophy, the report advised that the U.S. and IMF should "press Iraq to continue reducing subsidies in the energy sector . . . until Iraqis pay market prices for oil products," a proposal which, if implemented, would likely bring about massive disorder in a country where there was little consumer access to gasoline in the first place.

Shortly after the Baker-Hamilton report was released, a final draft of the proposed new Iraqi oil law was translated and leaked to outside observers.[160] It called for a federal oil and gas council that would rely on direct advice from an "independent consultants' bureau" including global oil companies.[161] During a transitional two-year period, the authority over ownership, management, and operations of existing fields would pass from the national oil company to the new council, which from then forward would make decisions on "not yet developed" fields. Since most of Iraq's seventy-three known oil fields are not yet developed, control over them would include direct participation by the American majors.[162]

[159] *The Iraq Study Group Report*, pp. 84–5.
[160] Leaked draft legislation translated by Raed Jarrar, February 21, 2007 (http://raedinthemiddle.blogspot.com/).
[161] See Article 5C of the draft legislation, cited in Jarrar.
[162] Juan Gonzalez, "Oily Truth Emerges in Iraq," *New York Daily News*, February 21, 2007. See also, Article 6 of the draft legislation, cited in Jarrar.

Between the lines, it appeared to be a plan for replacing American combat troops with oil company technicians.

But there was another major difference with 1968, the year that LBJ took the advice of his Wise Men and resigned the presidency. The Bush-Cheney White House, along with a dwindling number of neoconservative hardliners, were prepared to fight back.

CHAPTER 3

WHAT NOBLE CAUSE?
THE RISE OF THE ANTIWAR MOVEMENT, 2001–2007

M any observers, even some with long backgrounds of activism, hold the view that there has not been a significant peace movement against the war in Iraq. They range from the conservative John Mueller, who claims that peace movements are not responsible for public opinion turning against the war more quickly than during the Vietnam War; to the radical thinker Mike Davis, who bemoaned how the "spontaneous" 2003 movement was first "absorbed" by Howard Dean and finally "dissolved" by the John Kerry campaign of 2004.

Both these views, one by a national security expert and the other by a respected radical thinker (and good friend), are influenced by paradigms of the '60s with little relevance to the present antiwar opposition. Both define a movement as radical resistance against the established system, a view colored by templates and images of the militant confrontations of that earlier era. Both views are driven by ideology—in one case that national security should be the province of the elites, and in the other that a genuine movement should confront the system as a whole from the streets. Compared to 1916, 1938, 1968, and 1972, Davis argues, "voter opposition to foreign intervention [during the Iraq War] was not buttressed by an organized peace movement capable of holding politicians' feet to the fire or linking opposition to the war to a deeper critique of foreign policy."[1] Both these writers ignore hundreds of thousands of people who continue to protest the war.

Many unaffiliated progressives share these views, which are also prevalent among the students I teach. The long arm of the draft no longer invades their privacy. Their professors teach classes that never would have been allowed in the 1960s. They can vote and make at least a modest difference. They don't worry much about the police splitting their skulls. When and if they do go to peace marches, they are often turned off by the speeches. Everything in this freer society reinforces their sense of unimportance. As C. Wright Mills might have said, their personal contexts are detached from, or brushed ever so lightly by, the larger forces of politics and history where decisions are made about their lives.

And yet many of them still march, often with their parents from the 1960s generation.

In this chapter, I argue that the question is *how*, not whether, the peace movement participated in shaping antiwar opinion between 2003–07. The numbers of anti–Iraq War protesters in the streets—100,000–500,000 at least eight times in five years, plus ten million globally on one occasion—are comparable to the numbers during the 1965–68 period of Vietnam. Mueller, Davis, and others arbitrarily exclude electoral campaigns from their definition of movements; but if one considers the grassroots participation in the Dean, Kerry, Kucinich, Lamont, and other local campaigns, plus antiwar ballot initiatives in San Francisco, Chicago, and Vermont; and if one adds 165 city council resolutions passed against this war within a broader definition of "movement," then this has been a movement of historic proportions.

[1] Mike Davis, "The Democrats After November," *New Left Review*, January/February 2007.

As for the lack of an overarching critique of the system, I don't believe that radical ideological perspectives are gifts from intellectuals to activist movements. All social movements are built around core demands, and the recalcitrant nature of the system is revealed by experience, discussion, and interpretation. In this sense, Iraq has been a classroom for activists and all Americans to learn, concretely, the lessons of war, the possibilities of opposition, and the ultimate limits of the system.

The fact that today's movement has not been led by a clearly visible left says more about the crippling problems within the American left than the nature of the peace movement. I was part of the New Left of the '60s, and remember how much more interested I was in the "new" than the "left." Over time, I found it necessary and incredibly useful to study some classics of the left, from Marx to Fanon, but never found it easy to link their theories with everyday practice. In the end, I watched the New Left devour itself in versions of Old Left ideology, just at the moment when the American mainstream was becoming more open than ever to radical ideas and criticism. While another New Left hasn't developed in recent years, the reappearance of smaller and older "vanguard" factions has sometimes been a problem for the peace movement as it tries to reach out to nonpolitical people of various strata.

Resolving the complex reasons for the vacuum on the left is beyond my immediate purpose, but those issues have not stopped legions of pragmatic New Left veterans from opposing this war from the streets or institutions where they are now perched. More important, the vacuum has been filled by a new generation of activists ranging from the Seattle street radicals to new labor organizers to the spreading netroots of web activism. Disdaining what they often perceive as the past follies of the left, these activists are more pragmatic and entre-preneurial but no less passionate, informed, articulate, and strategic than their pre-digital predecessors. Many of the new leaders are women, some of whose collective styles of leader-ship make them less visible to male observers.[2]

The result of the work of earlier movements is a wider space for activism in a system whose "inside" and "outside" boundaries are more porous than ever before. The '60s protests were more militant, more oppositional, more anti-electoral, but not because of the ideologies of the left. Rather, it was because we could be drafted but could not vote; at least thirty million Southern blacks and eighteen- to twenty-one-year-olds were structurally disenfranchised, by law. There was no access to the media, which is why the underground press was formed, an achievement far exceeded by the multimedia accomplish-ment of this generation. The authorities were more repres-sive, from uncomprehending administrators to bullying police officers and right-wing super-patriots. There is now a more open, participatory institutional process, from politics to uni-versities to the Internet.

The present peace movement's growth compares favor-

[2] CODEPINK was cofounded by Medea Benjamin, Jodie Evans, and Gael Mur-phy, in part to bypass the male-controlled factional organizations of the left. United for Peace and Justice, the largest antiwar coalition, is led by a woman, Leslie Cagan. The most visible new leader of the overall movement is Cindy Sheehan. The most original and brilliant writers about Iraq and globalization, I believe, are Naomi Klein and Arundahti Roy; Phyllis Bennis and Antonia Juhasz are among the top analysts. The publisher of America's most respected progressive (and consistently antiwar) magazine, the *Nation*, is Katrina vanden Heuvel. One of the most effective progressive websites is Arianna Huffington's *Huffington Post*. The congressional Out of Iraq Caucus is led by women, in-cluding representatives Maxine Waters, Barbara Lee, and Lynn Woolsey. The greatest targets of right-wing wrath have been the previously nonpolitical, Texas-based music group the Dixie Chicks, who were subjected to physical threats when their singer said in 2003 that she was ashamed of Bush. Their unapologetic song "Not Ready to Make Nice" has been perhaps the most defi-ant and popular statement of protest during the war.

ably to the '60s when one considers some larger differences. The public anxiety over September 11 was much more chilling in 2002 than fear of global Communism in 1963. In Vietnam, the American troop numbers in a draft army were nearly five times greater, and after three years the number of American dead were about seven times higher, than that of Iraq in 2007. American taxpayers carried the direct costs of Vietnam, whereas many Americans (at least the wealthy) received tax reductions even as the Iraq War escalated; it was designed and structured in part to minimize adverse impacts on domestic society.

Factoring in these differences makes the existence of an anti–Iraq War movement all the more remarkable.

So how might the movement be defined and further succeed? Not by street actions alone, though they are important persuaders and energy-builders. As noted, there have been at least eight protests of more than 100,000 since 2002. Even more protests, including more civil disobedience, lie ahead. But they are not enough.

The movement cannot be defined by politicians either, though candidates and congresspeople play important legitimizing and galvanizing roles, especially when the peace movement keeps the pressure on them. Binary choices like "the streets" versus "politics" are too limited. Viewing the peace movement as both an "inside" and "outside" phenomenon leads me to believe that its cumulative pressure is producing institutional cracks and fissures from below, finally *causing the pillars of the Iraq War policy to fall.*

The pillars necessary for maintaining the war include favorable public (and global) opinion, bipartisan political support, an ample supply of soldiers, steady recruitment of new soldiers, public and congressional monetary support, diplomatic support from allies with resources, and some level of moral reputation. As I will discuss in more detail in Chapter 4, an individual or small group can impact any of these pillars through steady work—by picketing in front of military recruiters, by refusing to vote for pro-war candidates, by informing others of the costs of war through e-mail lists, by protesting tax money funding torture, and so on. By all these measures, the growth of antiwar opinion in civil society is bringing these pillars down.

Having said this, I am aware of the limits of the new peace movement as well. Iraqis are dying every day, and American soldiers are being sacrificed in a quagmire. The peace movement alone seems unable to find ways to push enough moderates into active opposition unless the Bush Administration jolts them with an exceptional transgression. National mobilizations often feature speakers whose tone and messages seem designed to turn people away in the name of "radicalizing" them.[3] Personal and organizational rivalries never cease. The movement has been unable to enlist labor, fair trade, civil rights, and environmental groups beyond token support.

Mike Davis is right to emphasize "the widespread consciousness in communities of color that the interventions in Iraq and Afghanistan . . . are stealing critical resources from human needs in poorer inner cities and older suburbs, as well as putting immigrant communities under the shadow of disloyalty."[4] The war has largely been driven by whites since the beginning; as early as mid-2003, a plurality of Latinos surveyed said the removal of Saddam Hussein was not worth the

[3] According to a spokesperson of the ANSWER coalition, the primary purpose of demonstrations is to "radicalize" and "hook" new activists, not to end the war. See David D. Kirkpatrick and Sarah Abruzzese, "In March on Pentagon, Protesters Recall War Anniversaries," *New York Times*, March 18, 2007.

[4] Davis, "The Democrats After November," *New Left Review*, January/February 2007.

loss of American lives and black opposition was greater than two-thirds.[5] It is perhaps no accident that polls about the war since then have largely avoided identifying racial or ethnic backgrounds of the respondents. Davis's dream of an inter-racial antiwar coalition demanding attention to the domestic agenda remains an unrealized possibility.

Those concerns aside, it is important to develop a new and different model in considering the scale and effectiveness of today's antiwar resistance. It is instructive to first examine the dire situation of 2002.

AT THE MARGINS AFTER SEPTEMBER 11

The attacks of September 11, 2001 drove peace advocates to the absolute margins of American life and politics. Suddenly, the neoconservative agenda had become prophetic and mainstream; in September 2000, they had predicted it would take a "catastrophic and catalyzing event—like a new Pearl Harbor"—to win public support for their cause.[6] Most Americans were seeking revenge for the attacks and would back a war against the terrorists, wherever they were.

Dissent was aggressively discouraged. The neoconserva-

---

[5] Adam Nagourney and Janet Elder, "Hispanics Back Big Government and Bush, Too," *New York Times*, August 3, 2003. Latino opposition was forty-nine percent. Depending on the question, black opposition to the war ran from sixty-five to eighty-one percent.

[6] Project for the New American Century, "Rebuilding America's Defenses: Strategy, Forces and Resources for a New Century," September 2000. The Pearl Harbor reference, especially in the wake of September 11 the following year, incited a wave of questioning whether the terrorist attacks were staged or manipulated to put the U.S. on a war footing. No direct evidence of such a plot has been produced, but the suspicions continue among a substantial minority of Americans. What seems certain is that the president and National Security Adviser Condoleezza Rice were warned in advance of an al-Qaeda plan to fly airplanes into buildings, and took no emergency steps to deter such a scheme, claiming later that the information, from an August 6, 2001 classified memo, was not specific enough.

tives launched tirades against anyone who suggested that the causes of the attacks lay in U.S. Middle East policy. Such questioning, however rational, was denounced as "soft on terrorism" and "blaming America first," the equivalents of being "soft on Communism" during the Cold War. This is consistent with the long-held neoconservative view that violence and crime should simply be suppressed, not understood as symptoms of underlying causes.[7] Former White House spokesman Ari Fleischer warned all Americans to "watch what they say, watch what they do."[8] Much liberal opinion turned hawkish or cautious.

In this context, the Patriot Act was drafted and passed with little protest, giving the government significant new tools for surveillance and suppression. Then the war on Afghanistan was launched with the justification that the Taliban-dominated state in Kabul "harbored" the al-Qaeda cells responsible for September 11. Only one member of Congress, Representative Barbara Lee from Berkeley, voted against the September 14, 2001 resolution authorizing open-ended war by the executive branch.[9]

---

[7] James Q. Wilson, an influential conservative theorist, purported to demonstrate that crime has no underlying causes that can be affected by public policy. Converted to political rhetoric, it was said that conservatives were liberals who had been mugged. This view justified the "super-predator" doctrine which predicted a teenage crime wave based on birth rates, and which underlaid the tough-on-crime policies and prison expansions of the mid-'90s. Wilson extended his opinions to foreign policy and Iraq, claiming in 2006 that the media was at fault. The thesis was challenged empirically by sociologist Michael Males and law professor Franklin Zimring at the University of California, and eventually even by its original academic advocate, John DiIulio, who had a change of mind. After September 11, however, the same doctrine was projected externally to explain terrorism as a problem to be met with military suppression, not by "soft power" approaches. In its purest form, the argument is that domestic and global terrorism are essentially evil, and therefore have no underlying causes and are not subject to human intervention.

[8] White House Press Briefing, Office of the Press Secretary, September 26, 2001.

[9] The authorization committed "all necessary and appropriate force" against

Never in recent memory had voices of peace been so marginalized.

Nevertheless, there were small pockets of opposition. A few who lost loved ones in the September 11 tragedy formed a group known as September 11th Families for Peaceful Tomorrows, which advocated against further violence.[10] They borrowed the words of Reverend Martin Luther King Jr., who once declared that "wars are poor chisels for carving out peaceful tomorrows." CODEPINK launched their efforts with a strong presence right outside the White House.

In addition, two hundred people joined the first protest in Washington, D.C. on September 24. Two weeks later, an estimated 5,000 people demonstrated under the slogan, *Not in our name*. A committee of antiwar actors and artists was soon formed, including Sean Penn, Tim Robbins, Susan Sarandon, Mike Farrell, and Robert Greenwald; they were attacked viciously as "traitors" in the tabloids.

APRIL 2002: PROTEST EMERGING

Such voices at the margins would begin breaking into the mainstream in 2002, as attention started turning from the impact of September 11 to the U.S. preparation for an invasion of Iraq. A mosaic of movements—the so-called anti-globalization protesters against the World Trade Organization, traditional antiwar forces, many supporters of Palestinian rights, and others—brought 20,000 to the rainy streets of Washington

any nation, person, or entity the president determined to have "planned, authorized, committed, or aided" the September 11 attacks, or "harbored" such elements. More broadly, the language appeared to empower the president to act militarily "to prevent any future acts of international terrorism against the United States."

[10] See David Potorti with Peaceful Tomorrows, *September 11th Families for Peaceful Tomorrows: Turning Our Grief into Action for Peace* (RDV/Akashic Books, 2003).

in April 2002. Resistance to war was building, though it remained at the margins. Hundreds of people were detained or preemptively arrested at the time with little media or public clamor. It was an interim phase between the large-scale, anti–corporate globalization protests of Seattle in 1999 and the anti–Iraq War movement that would rise as the confrontation drew closer.

The anti-globalization (or global justice) movement, which had burst into the public domain with the unexpected shutdown of the WTO in Seattle in December 1999, faced a dilemma in 2002. Should it, and could it, merge with the burgeoning antiwar movement, or would it be more effective as a parallel effort? Should the movements be maintained as multi-issue or single-issue? From the perspective of short-term effectiveness, taking on additional issues might be considered "baggage" and strain the capacity of the organizers. For example, the American unions who strongly supported "fair trade" were ambivalent or neutral toward Iraq in 2002. (Their official stance would become antiwar in 2005, a major change of direction.)

Most activists realized, however, that the issues of Iraq and globalization were inseparable; war and privatization went together in a kind of militarized neoliberalism. This phenomenon would be difficult to reduce into a protest slogan, especially as troops began to die on the battlefield.

Other developments legitimized the budding movement in 2002, especially the beginnings of protest among American soldiers and their families in groups like Military Families Speak Out. In the tradition of Vietnam Veterans Against the War, these groups, however small at first, competed successfully to impact the narrative about soldiers and the peace movement. Being pro-soldier, they argued, meant preventing war if possible and bringing the troops home, not trying to honor the dead by killing more Americans and Iraqis. Further, a relatively mainstream peace effort called Win Without War was initiated to garner the support of the clergy, civil rights leaders, businesses, politicians, and even retired military commanders.

OCTOBER 2002: THE MEDIA DENIES A PROTEST OF 100,000

On October 11, 2002, twenty-one Senate Democrats, one Independent, and one Republican voted against the war authorization; 133 House members had voted against it the previous day. Less than three weeks later, more than 100,000 protesters took to the streets of Washington, and smaller rallies were held across the U.S., including 50,000 demonstrators in San Francisco. The protests were so surprising, apparently, that both the *New York Times* and National Public Radio (NPR) denied their scale. The *Times* and NPR both quoted unnamed organizers as being disappointed in the turnout, with the *Times* speculating that fears of a D.C. sniper kept people in their homes. Within days, pushed by public outcry, both the *Times* and NPR apologized for their reporting errors.[11]

[11] The *New York Times'* initial version by Lynette Clemetson said that only "thousands" participated and that the numbers were less than the organizers had anticipated. Three days later, the *Times* re-reported the news, increasing the number of demonstrators to between 100,000 and 200,000. A *Times* senior editor wrote an apologetic letter to protesters who had complained to the paper. As for NPR, reporter Nancy Marshall's eyewitness account on *All Things Considered* declared that "it was not as large as the organizers had predicted. They said there would be 100,000 here. I'd say there are fewer than 10,000." Shortly after, NPR posted an apology on its website. The media watchdog group Fairness and Accuracy in Reporting (FAIR) had mobilized more than 1,100 letters from citizens protesting the downplaying of the rally. See Lynette Clemetson, "Thousands March in Washington Against Going to War in Iraq," *New York Times*, October 27, 2002. For the revised figure, see Kate Zernike, "Rally in Washington Is Said to Invigorate the Antiwar Movement," *New York Times*,

The October 2002 actions also saw the birth of a broader activist coalition, United for Peace and Justice (UFPJ). This was an attempt to provide a popular outlet for antiwar sentiment, including options from civil disobedience to mass marches to public education. Beginning with about seventy-five local affiliates in 2002, the network would grow to 1,425 groups with an e-mail blast list of 75,000 by 2007, and would coordinate most of the ensuing eight demonstrations of more than 100,000 people.[12] The rough numbers were:

- October 28, 2002, Washington, D.C.: 100,000-plus
- February 15, 2003, New York City: 500,000-plus
- October 25, 2003, Washington, D.C.: 100,000
- March 20, 2004, New York City: 100,000
- August 29, 2004, New York City: 600,000
- September 24, 2005, Washington, D.C.: 300,000
- April 29, 2006, New York City: 300,000
- January 27, 2007, Washington, D.C.: 500,000-plus

A less-visible phenomenon of online activism was bursting forth at the same time. Formed in June 2002, the Vermont-based TrueMajority.org tripled its membership from 100,000 to 350,000, raised $1 million, and paid for antiwar advertisements from October through the March 2003 invasion.[13] MoveOn.org grew at a similar rate. This form of activism went beyond the 1960s opposition in both scale and immediacy. It would continue to spread.

The street demonstrations alone were comparable in number to those during 1965–68 of the anti–Vietnam War

October 30, 2002. See also, FAIR Action Alert, October 28, 2002 (http://www.fair.org/activism/npr-nyt-protests.html).
[12] Interview, Hani Khallil, UFPJ.
[13] Interview, Duane Peterson, TrueMajority executive director. TrueMajority was formed by ice-cream entrepreneur Ben Cohen.

movement, though lacking the same confrontational intensity. The February 2003 prewar protests were certainly larger than anything preceding the Vietnam conflict. In fairness, the massive Moratorium of late 1969, the student strikes after the Cambodian invasion of 1970, and the May Day street clashes of 1971 were larger (though not by much) and more militant (by far). But those took place four years *after* Johnson had invaded Vietnam, with more initial troops than the U.S. had sent to Iraq, at a time when public impatience with hypocrisy over the war was overflowing. Similar times may lie ahead.

February 2003: The Second Superpower— Public Opinion

Despite its superpower pretensions, the U.S. government felt obligated for political reasons to approach the United Nations in order to appease public opinion at home and its allies abroad, especially those represented on the United Nations Security Council. This became an opportunity for one of the largest, if not *the* largest, recorded mobilizations of dissent by a social movement in American and world history.

Public doubt was materializing not only in the U.S., but globally as well in the form of powerful antiwar, anti-empire social movements, especially in countries regarded as traditional U.S. allies. Leaders of the European governments were Machiavellians, too, former colonial powers one and all, but the U.S. was now working toward a "new world order" in which these Western nations would be relegated to perpetual satellite status in a "uni-polar," American-dominated globe. These countries could be drawn into wars or trade and environmental agreements that were against their perceived national interests, with little consultation. Their citizens could die in

American-instigated conflicts. They could become targets in the next terrorist episode. There was also the nagging matter of their voting constituencies, who harbored overwhelming suspicion of U.S. plans for Iraq and the "new Middle East," and believed they would suffer from a loss of sovereignty, limited as it already was, over their political and economic institutions. It was a contradiction of globalization that could not be smoothed over.

On February 15, 2003, protesters all over the world took to the streets demanding that their governments heed the public outcry and oppose any UN authorization for war. The turnout was impossible to dismiss. The *New York Times*, for at least that day, acknowledged at the top of page one that there were "two superpowers": the United States and global public opinion.[14] This affirmation, unprecedented in the history of journalism, reflected the facts on the ground (and perhaps the *Times'* own editorial preference to delay the invasion).

People protested in at least 800 locations across the world.[15] In New York, South African Bishop Desmond Tutu delivered a message to UN Secretary-General Kofi Annan at a demonstration of a half-million people near the United Nations. In Montreal, where the weather was twenty degrees below zero, 200,000 people turned out. In countries where governments were considering sending troops to Iraq (the United Kingdom, Spain, Italy, Germany, etc.), the numbers neared the one million mark. People demonstrated on all continents, including at McMurdo Station in Antarctica.[16]

Iraq was the focal point of a new debate over the fair dis-

---

[14] Patrick E. Tyler, "A New Power in the Streets," *New York Times*, February 17, 2003.

[15] For a vivid and informative portrayal of the day's events, see Phyllis Bennis, *Challenging Empire: How People, Governments and the UN Defy U.S. Power* (Olive Branch Press, 2006).

[16] Bennis, pp. 258–61.

tribution of power in the world following the demise of the Soviet Union and the first Gulf War. Generally, there were three competing agendas:

- First, a *uni-polar* globe, sometimes called *empire* by friends and foes, dominated by the United States, was the objective of Bush Administration members like Donald Rumsfeld, who expressed the desire to "help discipline the world," according to Bob Woodward.[17] In this model, the U.S. would possess unassailable military power, would exploit the largest percentage of global resources, and would act as an economic superpower through its influence over the International Monetary Fund, the World Bank, the WTO, and other institutions. Free trade (the privatization of economies) would be integrated into official national security strategies. It was a conscious policy to prevent any future military or economic equivalence from competitors like the emerging European Union and nations like China.[18]

- Second, the vision of a *multi-polar world* was promoted by many countries that envisioned themselves as more than subservient satellites of the U.S. The shifting power "poles" in this model would vary, but would certainly include the European Union, Russia, China, India, Iran, South Africa, and a Latin Ameri-

[17] Bob Woodward and Dan Balz, "'We Will Rally the World': Bush and His Advisers Set Objectives, but Struggled with How to Achieve Them," *Washington Post*, January 28, 2002.
[18] The only other bloc aspiring to something like the status of empire is al-Qaeda and its supporters who seek, or at least dream of, the restoration of the caliphate through the reawakening and empowerment of the world's one billion Muslims.

can bloc including Venezuela and Brazil. In another form, the Non-Aligned Movement which grew out of the Cold War still consists of 118 member states, mostly in the global south. The UN General Assembly is yet another forum for these aspirations. Iraq and the Arab League, until the war was launched, had been key supporters of such a worldview as well. From this perspective, the UN and its related entities provide the space for negotiated approaches to global problems of peace and security, inequality and development, and environmental crises. In a multi-polar future, multinational corporations would be held accountable to codes developed by UN bodies, as originally conceptualized during the creation of the UN in the 1940s.

• Third, *a participatory model* of global decision-making was embedded in the voices, marches, and online activism of social movements themselves. Most nations already recognize non-governmental organizations as a sector providing a range of services, expertise, and advocacy, but they are nearly always limited to advisory roles. Social movements are the lifeblood of many NGOs, which otherwise atrophy into unaccountable bureaucracies often dependent on governments and corporations for funding. In the participatory model, the movements are a force beyond tax-exempt advocacy groups. They pressure governments and corporations directly, rather than through the mediation of political parties, eventually creating global *norms* that can turn into regulations, laws, and enforceable treaties. The evolving infrastructure of codes around human rights and global warming are two examples where decentralized movements have affected state and global institutions from the outside.

This three-dimensional paradigm of how power should be wielded globally is obviously in flux. The crucial force shaping this balance in 2002 was that of the "second superpower," or global public opposition to the Iraq War. So great was its force that it thwarted the U.S. expectation that the United Nations Security Council would authorize the invasion. The U.S. government went to great lengths to secure UN authorization, from wiretapping the private conversations of Security Council diplomats to suggesting military or economic "consequences" depending on how member states voted. Non-permanent members of the Security Council (i.e., Mexico, Chile, Angola, Cameroon, Guinea, and Pakistan) faced severe pressure from the U.S., including the possible loss of trade and investment packages they desperately needed.[19] As in Europe, however, public opinion in those countries ran powerfully against the war—over seventy percent in Mexico and eighty percent in Chile.[20]

Social movements succeeded in pressuring their governments to refuse a UN authorization for war. On the very day of the great march, February 15, 2003, the Associated Press reported:

Rattled by an outpouring of antiwar sentiment, the United States and Britain began reworking a draft resolution Saturday to authorize force against Saddam Hussein. Diplomats, speaking on condition of anonymity, said the final

[19] Tom Zeller, "How to Win Friends and Influence Smaller Countries," *New York Times*, March 16, 2003.
[20] William Schneider, "A Worldwide Tide of Anti-Bush Feeling," *Atlantic Monthly*, March 18, 2003.

product may be a softer text that does not explicitly call for war.[21]

The movement had succeeded in denying an important cloak of legitimacy to the bloody attack that was to follow, framing the war as shunned by world opinion and governing bodies. The United States, unable to win UN backing (or NATO support, for that matter), covered its unilateralism in a fragile and transparent "coalition of the willing" that the White House claimed had reached forty-nine countries, in various capacities, funded almost entirely by the U.S.[22] So unpopular was the war, globally, that the U.S. augmented its force with private mercenaries, whose numbers eventually reached 100,000.[23]

The term "global public opinion" does not adequately account for the spontaneous antiwar unity that occurred in 2003, and organizational concepts like "networking" cannot explain the scale of the emerging movement. This antiwar sentiment grew directly from legacies and memories rooted in civil society itself, not from organized resistance alone. Amateur plane-spotters exposed the thousands of secret "renditions" of prisoners to torture chambers carried out by the CIA and its allies. The first photographs of coffins bearing dead American troops arriving on U.S. soil appeared on the Internet. Grotesque images from Abu Ghraib prison were leaked by an individual American soldier. The top-secret national security state could not protect itself from creative, individual acts of conscience.

---

[21] "U.S., Britain Rework UN Resolution," Associated Press, February 15, 2003.

[22] "Coalition Members," White House Press Release, March 27, 2003.

[23] Renae Merle, "Census Counts 100,000 Contractors in Iraq," *Washington Post*, December 5, 2006.

165 Cities for Peace

On the home front, activists were turning their attention to local government officials, attempting to broaden and validate their cause by passing antiwar resolutions. Little noticed by the media, some 165 cities passed nonbinding resolutions condemning the war, including such diverse places as New York, Los Angeles, Chicago, Atlanta, Seattle, and Cleveland.[24] Many mayors and city council members flew to Washington to lobby their congressional delegations. In the process, activists were building new coalitions, testing and adjusting their messages to the mainstream, proving that peace politics were electorally viable, and challenging congresspeople through local constituencies.

More militant war opponents were adopting tactics of direct action and resistance, designed to increase radical consciousness and destabilize the structures of power. Resembling the SDS call *from protest to resistance* in 1967, these movements were fiercely effective in the Bay Area, where protesters laid nonviolent siege to downtown business districts and war profiteers like Bechtel and Halliburton. The police response was sometimes brutal.

Smaller, nonviolent, guerrilla-like actions were carried out by new groups like CODEPINK and Global Exchange, who unfurled protest banners in the midst of political conventions, congressional hearings, and press conferences. Adopting theatrical tactics to catch media attention, CODEPINK dressed in pink, held banners in pink, handed "pink slips" to pro-war politicians including Hillary Clinton, and sustained their own counterculture movement in difficult times—borrowing their organizational name from the various terrorist

---

[24] The "Cities for Peace" efforts started at the Institute for Policy Studies, a venerable Washington, D.C. think tank founded in 1963.

alert codes used by the Department of Homeland Security, and branding those codes with a feminist twist. Over 1,000 CODEPINK activists were arrested in various protests and its online membership grew to 120,000 by 2007.[25]

Whether or not these direct action approaches changed any minds, they at least became a nuisance to the powerful, without adverse repercussions from the public, and served to attract, educate, and involve a new generation of activists in the political process. Instead of waiting in vain for the state to beat and arrest them on television, they embarked on a nonviolent offensive and moved directly to contest and claim public space.

The *success* of this movement was to delegitimize the Machiavellian faction who sought war at any cost. The *perceived failure* was its inability to prevent the war. The *outcome* was a periodic disillusionment and decline of the movement, as when the U.S. government inflicted "shock and awe" on Iraq on March 20, 2003, causing public support for the war to increase. "It was a profoundly emotional run-up to the attack," said a TrueMajority organizer, "and people were really deflated after it began anyway."[26]

The media largely stopped covering antiwar voices after the invasion, a pattern that has persisted. The antiwar movement continues to exist, however, in small networks around the country, despite being marginalized in national discourse. Its future depends not on media attention, but on the length of the war and the moral reaction of people in local communities.

Polling data is somewhat unreliable, and gauging any causal relationship between antiwar activism and public opinion is difficult. But to deny *any* impact of antiwar protest on public opinion, as Mueller did in his *Foreign Affairs* article,

[25] Interview, Jodie Evans, cofounder of CODEPINK.
[26] Interview, Duane Peterson, TrueMajority executive director.

makes no sense whatsoever. Since the media was overwhelmingly pro-war, as evidenced by generals and intelligence experts serving as round-the-clock television commentators during the period of invasion,[27] where did the public receive its critical information except from antiwar sources and memories of Vietnam?

A combination of factors began to influence public opinion. The first and most obvious were signs by mid-2003 that the expected quick victory was not materializing. The second was that public opinion had been "prepared" for a critical alternative, as it were, by months of congressional debate, the UN rejection, and the ensuing massive demonstrations. Third, since the 1999 Seattle protests, social movements had developed phenomenal communication abilities through independent progressive media and the Internet. This latter trend was exemplified by the netroots, an extraordinary culture of online activists with outlets of their own, including daily radio broadcasts by *Democracy Now!*, potent new blog sites, and political advocacy by organizations like MoveOn and TrueMajority.

But as discussed in Chapter 1, something deeper was also

---

[27] These pro-war television narrators of the invasion included: [1] ABC: Tony Cordesman, security analyst; Lieutenant General Gregory Newbold, director of operations, Joint Chiefs of Staff, 2000–02; Richard Hawley, former head of Air Combat Command; General Charles Horner, air commander of Desert Shield and Desert Storm; Christopher Meyer, former British ambassador; Richard Clarke, counterterrorism chief under Clinton; Jack Cloonan, FBI specialist on Osama bin Laden; [2] CBS: Stephen Black, UN weapons analyst; General Buck Kernan, commander in chief, Joint Forces Command, 2000–02; General Joseph Ralston, supreme allied commander, Europe/NATO; [3] NBC: General Barry McCaffrey, chief of U.S. Southern Command; General Norman Schwarzkopf, commander, Desert Shield and Desert Storm; [4] FOX: Ambassador Dennis Ross, Middle East negotiator under Clinton; Lieutenant Colonel Tim Eads, investigator of the bombing of U.S. barracks in Saudi Arabia; Lieutenant Colonel Bill Cowan, head of Pentagon's classified counterintelligence unit; [5] CNN: General Wesley Clark, former NATO commander; Major General David Grange, former commander of "Big Red One"; [6] PBS: Colonel John Warden, air force Gulf War architect; W. Patrick Lang, former director, Defense Intelligence Agency. See Elizabeth Jensen, "Networks' War Strategy: Enlist Armies of Experts," *Los Angeles Times*, March 18, 2003.

affecting American consciousness: the Vietnam Syndrome. A whole generation of Americans, now in their middle years and older, had heard the current administration's refrains before, during a traumatic and transformative period of their lives. They—we—had learned the hard way that presidents and governments lie to start wars, that they institutionalize their lies through intelligence agencies and security classifications, that promises of easy victory underestimate the strength of the Other. These latent suspicions reemerged as the invasion of Iraq showed few signs of success in 2003. The syndrome had survived all government and media inoculation, and began to serve as a major source of public doubt.

The shift in public opinion was a gradual process, but discernible in surveys conducted by the *Washington Post*/ABC News in that first year.[28] In June 2003, according to polls, the public thought the war was "worth fighting," by 64-33 percent. The numbers dipped by November to 52-44, then held at year's end at 59-33. This public support would crumble, however, as the WMD allegations proved to be false and the war became a true quagmire.[29]

Similarly, the public initially believed that the war was "contributing to long-term security" by an overwhelming margin of 62-34 percent. This notion would diminish, too, as the situation in Iraq steadily devolved.

In April 2003, when the insurgency was barely underway, the public felt that American casualties were acceptable by a ratio of 66-28. But by the year's end, when American deaths approached 500, only thirty-seven percent of the public felt the losses were acceptable; a disconnect between the deaths

[28] All polling data referred to here is from the *Washington Post*/ABC News poll, December 12, 2006 (http://www.washingtonpost.com/wp-srv/politics/polls/postpoll_121206.htm).
[29] In my blog, I first wrote, "Say It: This Is a Quagmire," on July 7, 2003. See *AlterNet* (http://www.alternet.org/story/16336/).

of our troops and what plausible purpose they were serving was beginning to appear to the American public. The Iraq Syndrome was surfacing.

HOWARD DEAN AS EUGENE MCCARTHY REBORN

As I have said, an *outside-inside model* is needed to understand the full scope of social movements. These movements can be *catalytic* in several ways. They can create a climate and space that makes politicians and the media more likely to address previously ignored issues. They can challenge systems to reform or face dissent, defections, disorder, and defeat. As they gain momentum and scale, movements can expand beyond the streets and into the political process.

In 1967–68, this was the case with the presidential campaign of Senator Eugene McCarthy. McCarthy offered himself as a candidate to end the war, reform the political system through empowering a new constituency, and at the same time prevent deepening domestic instability. I remember seeing him for the first time stepping off an elevator into the cramped and disorderly offices of an antiwar group in New York. For many of us, he was the first tie-wearing official who had ever reached out to us. I preferred Robert Kennedy as a candidate, and he also enjoyed tremendous support from black and Latino communities. But I doubted that either McCarthy or Kennedy would end the war without an angry tide of American public opinion. Most of my friends at that point perceived them as wanting to co-opt the antiwar movement by bringing it safely within the electoral system. Their increasingly radical path was threatened by the safer and broader electoral alternative, although a tacit consensus tolerating divergent approaches would emerge. Growing talk of radical resistance seemed to in fact quicken support for reformist alternatives.

While Kennedy held back, McCarthy plunged ahead, thus earning the dedicated, even dogmatic allegiance of a youthful army comparable to the MoveOn and netroot constituencies of this generation. McCarthy perceived what no other conventional candidate did: that there was a yearning to end the Vietnam War through the practical path of electoral politics. Thousands of young people tramped through the snows of New Hampshire and helped achieve a stunning upset in the first 1968 Democratic primary. Public disillusionment with the Vietnam War, combined with idealistic door-knockers, resulted on March 12 in a forty-two percent result for McCarthy in New Hampshire, against Johnson's forty-nine percent.[30]

A sitting wartime president had been denied a majority in his own party's primary. This shocking event propelled Robert Kennedy into the race on March 16, and contributed to Johnson's withdrawal. McCarthy ultimately lost in 1968, winning only twenty-three percent of the convention delegates, but he helped create a progressive wing of the Democratic Party that lasted for a generation. It is also true, as the radical critics warned, that many of the McCarthy volunteers would evolve later into the centrist and sometimes hawkish political circles of politicians like Bill and Hillary Clinton.[31] When pragmatic radicals become insiders, the road to unconscious opportunism is opened, and the challenge of electoral politics gradually reshapes original belief systems. But that is not to ignore the

[30] Richard Corliss, "Eugene McCarthy: 1916–2005," *Time*, December 12, 2005.
[31] The Clintons themselves were involved in the 1972 George McGovern presidential campaign. Among the McCarthy activists of 1968, many would go on to join the Clinton Administration, among them John Podesta, Sandy Berger, Geoff Cowan, Harold Ickes, Mary Louise Oates, and others. McCarthy's press secretary was Seymour Hersh, who quit the campaign and later became the most distinguished investigative reporter of our generation.

McCarthy volunteers' impact on the war when other politicians remained silent.

In this sense, Howard Dean was the Eugene McCarthy of 2003. The growing impatience of the antiwar movement flowed into Dean's presidential campaign, which was triggered by his impertinent statement at a National Democratic Committee meeting in 2003, questioning why the Democratic Party wasn't opposing the war in Iraq. Until then, Dean had been governor of a tiny and largely white New England state, making the rounds in Iowa with a lone and loyal staffer. Immediately after raising the Iraq question, however, his campaign was flooded with volunteers and money, at historic levels.

Much has been made of the netroots in fueling the Dean campaign, and deservedly so. As with many innovations in social movements, it came "out of nowhere," in the narrative of campaign manager Joe Trippi:

> We had no idea what was happening. This hadn't come from us. This had come from out there. Out there, the original e-mail [asking for $25 and a penny] was being picked up and posted on blogs and websites and the money was flying in. By the end of the quarter, about $400,000 had come in with pennies attached.[32]

The average Dean contribution was only $100, but in a single day, June 27, 2003, donors sent in a half-million dollars.[33] In the end, the Dean campaign raised $50 million in contributions from 600,000 supporters; his Meetup.com site rapidly grew from 432 to 190,000 members.[34] He picked up

[32] Joe Trippi, *The Revolution Will Not Be Televised: Democracy, the Internet, and the Overthrow of Everything* (Regan Books, 2004), p. 106.
[33] Trippi, p. 131.
[34] Trippi, p. 86.

roughly 400,000 activist supporters in the MoveOn web presidential primary, who raised him some $25 million.[35] He rose to first in the presidential polls, but only took twenty-six percent in the New Hampshire primary and eighteen percent in Iowa before being stopped. Dean served as an unprecedented threat to the incumbent hierarchy of the Democratic Party. But the campaign had only been possible because the antiwar movement needed an outlet for rising public anger over Iraq. Dean would have gone nowhere if he had campaigned solely on his Vermont health care plan.

But Dean's criticism was of the "premature" decision to go to war, never a clarion call to withdraw. He viewed his candidacy as part of a pragmatic process that would culminate in an unspecified end of the war. Many stalwart antiwar activists found their candidate in Representative Dennis Kucinich, whose call for speedy withdrawal was linked to proposals for a shift to nonviolent conflict resolution. This appealed to the moral values of his constituency. Reflecting the pragmatism of Dean's antiwar constituency—that is, their desire to end the war simply by defeating Bush—the feistier Kucinich campaign never drew much support beyond one percent. Dean said of his volunteers that they were "more mature, less confrontational, more effective than our ['60s] generation. We were very confrontational, fighting the entire establishment, while this generation didn't have to do that so much."[36]

Dean's sudden demise in Iowa, however, reflected another dilemma that sets in when movements commingle in institutional politics. The desire to win becomes paramount over issues. Machiavellian politics, after all, is about preserving incumbent power. Dean was not only challenging the Democratic national security hawks on Iraq, he was disrupting the

[35] Interview, Tom Matzzie, political director, MoveOn.
[36] Interview, Howard Dean.

status quo fabric of the party organization. I remember a dinner discussion in late 2003 with experienced operatives from past Democratic campaigns. "When are the adults going to get into this?" asked one. He was implying that the party couldn't afford to be dominated by idealistic Dean volunteers. These experienced party professionals finally coalesced against Dean in Iowa, and after his support imploded following the Iowa primary, the establishment had won. According to Dean himself, the establishment hadn't interceded, although a "ton of money" and other offers had been tendered toward him. Al Gore, who had endorsed Dean, talked him through the options. Gore "wasn't representing any establishment," Dean felt, but they shared the view that quitting the race was the "right thing to do."[37]

The irony is that the party pros went to work for Senator John Kerry, a candidate who had plenty of experience but little understanding of the fervent rank and file, and who proceeded to lose narrowly in a contest dominated by the competing memories of 1960s social movements. Afterwards, Dean's constituency successfully elected him party chairman, signaling the recognition that a new grassroots phenomenon had emerged.

The issue of Iraq remained paramount in the 2004 election, despite the wishes and predictions of pundits from both parties. While Bush won by a paper-thin margin, the country as a whole was flooded with information and debate, most of it damning to the war policies. Among the key developments:

• Iraq Veterans Against the War was formed in July 2004, strengthening the antiwar movement with the

---

[37] I found Dean's explanation hard to believe. His collapse in Iowa forced him to quit to avoid a greater disaster. It also salvaged the possibility that he could campaign later for party chairman, a path not taken by McCarthy.

support of military families. No such pro-war veterans' voice emerged outside the White House and conservative talk-radio hosts. The first war resisters appeared in Canada, seeking asylum from the U.S. military, as happened in large numbers during Vietnam.

• For the first time, a grassroots movement of antiwar union activists gained the endorsement of the AFL-CIO, long an accomplice of the neoconservatives and even the CIA in American foreign policy.[38]

• Huge protests were mounted at the 2004 Republican National Convention in New York City, despite government efforts to sabotage or diminish the turnout through surveillance of antiwar groups, fabricated threats of terrorism at the convention, and refusal to grant permits for a mass rally in Central Park. In the end, several hundred thousand demonstrators turned out, once again a confluence of older and younger generations of activists.[39] It was the largest protest in the history of American political conventions. The numbers arrested, nearly all in police sweeps, totaled 1,800, also the largest in the history of conventions, and three times greater than the historic 1968 Chicago Democratic Convention demonstrations. The street resistance to Bush's policies was undertaken almost entirely by movement activists rather than Democratic politicos, who may have worried about fallout if events turned ugly. The inner logic and sophistication

[38] "Labor Coalition Opposes War with Iraq," CNN, February 28, 2003.
[39] Graham Rayman, Lindsay Faber, Daryl Kahn, and Karen Freifeld, "Massive Protest Mostly Peaceful," Los Angeles Times, August 30, 2004.

of the movement was revealed in its choice *not* to orchestrate significant protests outside the Democratic convention that same summer, although the FBI and police issued the predictable warnings of a possible "anarchist invasion."[40]

• Online activism mushroomed, as progressive blogs averaged five million readers a day at the height of the 2004 campaign season, to twenty times the size of its 2003 audience.[41] Of the $60 million MoveOn spent during the 2004 election, its voter fund alone raised $20 million, an amount never spent by a peace group on an election in American history. And according to FEC filings, MoveOn members donated more than $180 million to Democratic candidates.[42]

• Related to the success of online activism was the phenomenal distribution of Robert Greenwald's antiwar documentaries, *Unprecedented: The 2000 Presidential Election* and *Uncovered: The War on Iraq*, which were widely circulated as DVDs among tens of thousands

---

[40] Mike Davis is right in disparaging the 2004 Democratic convention as a celebration of Kerry as a "Brahmin Rambo," but off-mark in attacking the movement for "politically dissolving" into the Kerry campaign. The history of Ralph Nader's 2000 campaign, which to many played a part in the defeat of Al Gore, weighed heavily on movement activists in 2004. They held a social forum but almost no protests at the Boston convention, focusing their resources on the street protests the following month at Bush's convention. Kerry's ambivalence toward the war, plus his lack of emphasis on his own antiwar past, disappointed thousands of activists who nonetheless worked on the campaign. The feeling was first to dump Bush, second to claim a victory for the antiwar movement, and third to hold massive demonstrations during Kerry's inauguration. Alternatives like "taking to the streets" simply did not resonate with many people during those months, again showing the tendency in protest movements to address the immediate opportunity for change.

[41] Chris Bowers, "The Role of the Netroots in Democratic Victories," *Democratic Strategist*, April 2007.

[42] Interview, Tom Mattzie.

of Americans who used them as organizing tools in house meetings.[43]

• Meanwhile, *Democracy Now!'s* "War and Peace Report" provided critical information on a daily basis to a global audience, including up to 40,000 radio listeners every morning in Los Angeles alone.[44] Three million would become regular listeners of *The Ed Schultz Show* on the progressive Air America radio network.[45]

• On a grander and unexpected scale came the documentary work of Michael Moore, who had started as an alternative muckraker and rose to "make it" in mainstream film and television. In 2004, Moore obliterated any clear distinction between outsider and insider with *Fahrenheit 9/11*, the largest grossing documentary in film history. Half the American people said they planned to see the film at home or in theaters.[46] The Walt Disney Company refused to distribute the film, which was attacked vociferously by the White House and conservative talk-show hosts. Partly because of the controversy, merely attending a screening became a form of protest, and *Fahrenheit 9/11* had the biggest opening day for any film at several New York cine-

---

[43] According to Greenwald's production company, Brave New Films, nearly thirty-five thousand DVDs of *Uncovered* were sold and distributed through MoveOn in a two-day spree in 2004. An estimated 100,000 were sold through all outlets over the following year.

[44] According to Allen Minsky, the estimated 250,000 weekly listeners to *Democracy Now!* were "the greatest number in the long history of the station." Interview, KPFK, Los Angeles.

[45] Sean Mitchell, "The Talk Gets Heated," *Los Angeles Times*, April 6, 2007.

[46] Seven percent of the filmgoers were Republican (another ten percent of Republicans were "extremely" or "very" likely to see it), and forty-four percent of them said they would recommend the movie to other Republicans. Harris poll, July 23, 2004.

mas, ran in theaters for sixteen weeks, grossed $220 million, and won the top prize at the Cannes Film Festival. According to Moore, polling showed that *Fahrenheit 9/11* was influencing independent voters in crucial presidential battlegrounds. The film's impact went beyond the wildest dreams of the underground and independent media counterculture that Moore, and his wife Kathleen Glynn, belonged to.

• In Iraq itself, the most significant impact on American opinion came in 2004 when photographs were made public of monstrous scenes of detainee abuse at Abu Ghraib prison outside Baghdad. Though CBS broadcast the photos on April 28, they might never have been seen without being leaked.[47] The International Red Cross had been documenting human rights violations at Abu Ghraib throughout 2003, but their reports had been kept confidential from the American people.[48] It was from an individual in civil society, not responsible officials, that the truth was revealed. The negative impact of the torture and cover-up on global and American opinion was pervasive: Added to the loss of lives and tax dollars was the price of America's reputation.

---

[47] In January 2004, specialist Joseph Darby turned over CDs with hundreds of photos to the army's Criminal Investigation Command (CID). Results of the subsequent inquiry were leaked to the *Washington Post*, perhaps by the relative of a military policeman. See Mark Danner, *Torture and Truth: America, Abu Ghraib, and the War on Terror* (New York Review of Books, 2004), pp. 215–16.

[48] An army general testified to Congress that the confidential reports were "lost in the army's bureaucracy and never adequately addressed." According to the *New York Times*, the army tried to curtail the Red Cross' spot inspections of the prison. The Red Cross report was leaked to the *Wall Street Journal* in May 2004. See Danner, pp. 215–16.

By the end of 2004, according to the *Washington Post*, just forty-two percent of Americans thought that the Iraq War was "worth fighting," compared with fifty-nine percent twelve months before. The numbers in favor of keeping our troops there dropped from seventy-two percent in July 2003 to fifty-eight percent by December 2004 (with those favoring immediate withdrawal rising from twenty-six to thirty-nine percent). The ratio of those believing American casualty rates were "acceptable" versus "unacceptable" went from 37-60 percent in December 2003 to 27-70 percent in December 2004, a major shift despite Bush's November reelection.[49]

EARLY 2005: A ROUGH PERIOD FOR THE MOVEMENT

Having invested so much in the unsuccessful effort to defeat Bush, the antiwar movement suffered a profound disillusionment in the weeks after the 2004 presidential election. Most of the movement had suspended its skepticism toward electoral politics and many had thrown themselves into campaigning for Kerry. This was a reversal from 2000, when thousands had worked for Ralph Nader in an attempt to bring a social movement directly into electoral politics at the national level. In addition, millions of Americans were jolted by the perception that the 2000 election had been stolen.

In 2004, most in the movement tried to avoid making the same mistakes. Whatever Kerry's flaws, the election was perceived as a referendum on Bush, and if Kerry had been elected, he would have become president amidst rising expectations for peace in Iraq. Protests would likely have continued in the streets after his inauguration. But the 2004 loss plunged many into despair over the antiwar movement's lack of mate-

[49] *Washington Post*/ABC News poll, December 12, 2006.

rial success. The anguish went as deep as the energies that had been invested.

To make matters worse, leading Democrats, including Kerry and Dean, walked away from the Iraq issue for the next six months, enabling Bush to launch a bloody offensive in Fallujah and fight the insurgency without much domestic opposition.[50]

Even MoveOn drew back from the antiwar effort, causing me to send a letter reflecting the despair of 2005:

> MoveOn has been a true innovation with historical impacts and implications, no doubt about that. [But] MoveOn seems very much tied to the direction of the Democractic Party in its posture against the Republicans. That makes it difficult, perhaps impossible, to take on Democrats like Pelosi for their pro-war positions of the past six months, or the general Democratic view that Iraq was a mistake, but it would be a bigger mistake to withdraw (or that it was a mistake to invade, but now we have to win). The result is that the broad and independent antiwar movement can only rely on MoveOn where Republicans are the problem . . .
>
> Second, the very marketing/direct-mail philosophy which makes MoveOn successful can also make the organization go AWOL when the antiwar struggle hits a downturn, as during the past six months . . . The result is that MoveOn can be missing when times are really hard . . . The result is an unreliable partnership. You should consider whether to criticize pro-war Democrats and their silent partners . . . You should think of the independent

---

[50] Kerry defended the Fallujah offensive, signaling that Bush would have no Democratic opposition to worry about. Dean was silent. Another Democratic presidential candidate, retired General Wesley Clark, said there was no choice on Fallujah but to "take them out" (author interview, November 2004).

antiwar movement as your allies on Iraq, more than the
Democratic Party . . .[51]

I had also written Dean an angry public letter on April 26 deploring the party's "moral default" and arguing that the alliance with the peace movement, in repair since the 2000 split with Ralph Nader, was "unraveling" again. Here is an excerpt:

I am not suggesting that the Democratic Party has to sup-
port language favoring "out now" . . . What I am arguing
is that the Democratic Party must end its silent consent to
the Bush Administration's Iraq War policies and stand for
a negotiated end to the occupation and our military pres-
ence . . . Stop marginalizing those Democrats who are call-
ing for immediate withdrawal or a one-year timetable . . .

This is a familiar pattern for those of us who suffered
through the Vietnam War. Today it is conventional wisdom
among Washington insiders, including even the liberal me-
dia, that the Democratic Party must distance itself from
its antiwar past . . . The truth is quite the opposite. The
Democratic Party should distance itself from its immoral
and self-destructive pro-war positions in the 1960s which
led to unprecedented polarization, the collapse of funds for
the War on Poverty, a schism in the presidential primaries,
and the destruction of the Lyndon Johnson presidency . . .

Thirty years after our forced withdrawal from Viet-
nam, the U.S. government has stable diplomatic and com-
mercial relations with its former Communist enemy. The
same future is possible in Iraq.[52]

[51] Tom Hayden, "Letter to MoveOn," *Huffington Post*, June 24, 2005. See http://www.huffingtonpost.com/tom-hayden/letter-to-moveon-re-iraq_b_3158.html.
[52] Tom Hayden, "Open Letter to Howard Dean." See http://www.thenation.com/blogs/edcut?pid=2356.

I soon met with Dean at the Democratic National Committee headquarters. He recognized that bridges to the antiwar movement needed repair, and that criticism of the party's message was hardly unfounded. Since being forced out of his role as presidential candidate, he now found himself navigating between competing ideologies and power centers within the party, including a faction that still resented him. Dean also acknowledged what was readily apparent—that he himself was uncertain about the right path in Iraq. The demand for immediate withdrawal didn't satisfy him intellectually or politically, yet he and many other Democrats opposed "staying the course." The same ambivalence—criticizing Bush's management of the war but not the mission itself—had confounded Kerry, and perhaps lost him the presidency, a few months earlier.

There was an alternative, I suggested. The Democrats could call for public hearings on an exit strategy, an approach that appeared more "responsible" than simply pulling the plug. They could propose deadlines for withdrawing American troops and phasing in diplomatic and reconstruction initiatives, instead of maintaining the open-ended status quo. Dean agreed, and soon spoke to the House Progressive Caucus, encouraging them to step forward and initiate hearings of some kind. A thaw was beginning.

An ad hoc hearing was held in September, in procedural defiance of the Republicans controlling the House. It was sparsely attended, however, and mainly featured witnesses from the national security establishment. While the hearing may have opened an internal conversation regarding an exit strategy, it meandered in no particular direction.

Nevertheless, even in the worst of times, the tide was

beginning to turn toward peace. Beyond the corridors of a cautious Congress, a June 2005 Harris poll showed that sixty-three percent of Americans supported a one-year withdrawal timetable.[53] By early 2005, while U.S. combat deaths reached nearly 1,500 in Iraq, the percentage who believed the war was a mistake passed the fifty percent level, which had not occurred in the Vietnam era until the Tet Offensive of February 1968, after some 20,000 American deaths.[54] Something had changed.

After all the months of paralysis and despair, powerful antiwar spirits were about to rise again. I had been looking for hope from Congress, but I should have been looking toward Crawford, Texas.

AUGUST 2005: CINDY SHEEHAN'S PROTEST

The military families represented in Gold Star Families for Peace were different than many antiwar activists. Despite, or because of, their much deeper sorrow, they could not retreat from trying to end the war. In the suffocating, slow-news atmosphere of summer 2005, one of them, Cindy Sheehan, decided to travel to George Bush's Texas ranch and demand a meeting with the president. The media decided this was a story, and so, evidently out of nowhere, a new phase of the peace movement was born. Of course, such events only "arrive out of nowhere" when patient work, good timing, and the media's attention are aligned. A bit like Rosa Parks sitting in the whites-only section of a Montgomery bus, Cindy Sheehan sat down in the sweltering heat on the road to Bush's ranch and the whole world watched the spectacle unfold. A spontaneous and lasting community immediately formed around

[53] Harris poll, June 7–12, 2005.
[54] Mueller, "The Iraq Syndrome," *Foreign Affairs*.

her. Hundreds slept on the ground, held dialogues in open tents, and carried on a seemingly endless press conference. Although from Berkeley, Cindy Sheehan was apple pie, a mom whose grief was genuine and who expressed a question now shared by most Americans: *What was the "noble cause" her son Casey had died for?*

A younger John Kerry had posed a similar question—*How can you ask a soldier to be the last to die for a lie?*—at a similar turning point three decades before. Like Sheehan, he was a charismatic individual, more appealing to the media than the rowdier, ragtag radicals of his generation. Individuals like Kerry and Sheehan could be cast as American patriots in the tradition of John Ford movies—not troublemakers and traitors—who might save a system gone wrong. Both embodied a vital element in making the peace movement successful. They had "skin in the game," as some veterans say, meaning their suffering allowed them to offer a healing alternative to the national guilt over so many deaths in an unnecessary war.

Bush had no answer to Sheehan, leaving her in the ditch, a situation an increasing number of Americans identified with. In a national survey, a significant fifty-two percent said that Bush should meet with Cindy Sheehan and answer her question.[55] The antiwar movement had been restored in the public eye, not as a group of chronic complainers, but as an instrument to interrogate the powerful with a persistent question—*What noble cause?*—to which there was no answer.

"It really took Cindy Sheehan to breathe life back into us," recalls Duane Peterson, a spokesperson for TrueMajority. CODEPINK, TrueMajority, and MoveOn went to work, and in seven days, Peterson recalls, some 6,000 candlelight vigils were

[55] Richard Morin and Dan Balz, "President's Poll Rating Falls to a New Low," *Washington Post*, August 31, 2005.

organized across the country, involving hundreds of thousands of people. It was stunning in its immediacy and scale.

On September 24, 2005, a march of 300,000 in Washington, D.C., while harmed by factionalism, showed the revival of spirits, ending with the arrest of Sheehan and 300 others.

By November 2005, only twenty-five percent of Americans believed American casualty rates were "acceptable," while seventy-three percent took the side of mothers like Sheehan.[56]

In one of many parallels with Vietnam, George W. Bush began to experience his Watergate moment by the end of 2005. Selling a dubious and increasingly unpopular war required from the beginning a pattern of executive behavior that broke with public norms and the law itself. The Niger yellowcake scandal would not go away. Even more egregious, though less covered by the media, were prewar memos disclosed in 2005 showing that top British intelligence officials believed the president was "fixing the facts to fit the policy," potentially an impeachable crime.[57]

Next, Bush had found his version of Daniel Ellsberg, the discloser of the Pentagon Papers whom Richard Nixon had sent secret operatives to discredit. This time it was former Ambassador Joseph Wilson, who had written a *New York Times* op-ed dismissing the notion that Saddam Hussein sought yellowcake uranium from Niger.[58] In the Ellsberg case, Nixon's burglars stole personal files from a Beverly Hills therapist's office; in the Wilson case, his wife's identity as a clandestine CIA agent was leaked in violation of federal national security laws,

[56] *Washington Post*/ABC News poll, December 12, 2006.
[57] Full transcript, "The Secret Downing Street Memo," *Sunday Times* (U.K.), May 1, 2005.
[58] Joseph C. Wilson IV, "What I Didn't Find in Africa," *New York Times*, July 6, 2003.

and resulted in the successful prosecution of Vice President Cheney's top adviser.

The extreme penchant for secrecy, starting with Nixon and building to great heights with the Bush Administration, was based on fears of the democratic public. In 1974, House Democrats like Representative John Conyers participated in the joint impeachment hearings against Richard Nixon; by 2005, Conyers was drafting legislation to begin the impeachment process against Bush.

2006: THE MOVEMENT BECOMES A MAJORITY

The disaster of Hurricane Katrina in 2005 raised serious concerns about the *domestic* costs of the Iraq War. While Congress dithered, more Americans were making connections between Bush's policies at home and abroad. For the first time in a long while, the contours of a progressive link between foreign and domestic policy became apparent. Eighty-three percent of Americans were "very" (fifty-three percent) or "somewhat" (thirty percent) concerned that Iraq was costing "money and resources needed in the U.S." Ninety percent opposed cutting expenditures for health care or education to pay for Iraq.[59] The war was slowly coming home.

Then something happened—a delayed response, to be sure, but a more visible reaction in Congress to the festering public discontentment with the war, especially among rank-and-file Democrats. First, an Out of Iraq Caucus was formed by dissident Democrats, led by Representative Maxine Waters, over the initial concerns of House Democratic leader Nancy Pelosi. It would grow to over eighty members, one of the largest caucuses on the Hill.

[59] All data from a *New York Times*/CBS poll, September 9–13, 2005.

In November 2005, behind closed doors, the most hawk-ish senior member of the Democratic Caucus, a retired marine named John Murtha, rose to address his colleagues. Murtha, known to be close to marine commanders in Iraq, spoke as never before, expressing painful worry that U.S. soldiers were being lost in an unwinnable war. He advised the withdrawal of nearly all American troops in a six-month time frame. The caucus rose in a standing ovation.

Murtha's rebellion was not isolated. Little noticed at the time, Baghdad commander General George Casey had been drawing up plans for significant troop reductions, based partly on back-channel contacts with Sunni insurgents interested in political negotiations.[60] As Murtha's rhetoric was consistent with the plans of a ranking commander, Democrats could safely begin to discuss withdrawing troops. Polls and constitu-ent meetings showed party leaders that they had to break with the president's "stay the course" policies and begin aligning themselves with the frustrated antiwar constituency going into the 2006 midterm elections.

But any hope of troop withdrawals was derailed on Feb-ruary 22, 2006, when unknown saboteurs destroyed the al-Askariya Mosque in Samarra (see Chapter 2). It was a huge blow to the fragile possibilities for peace. Both the Democratic and Republican establishments desired to avoid discussing the war, if at all possible, through the 2006 elections. For Repub-lican strategists, it was a matter of loyalty to Bush's mission versus the demands of increasingly disgruntled constituents. On the same day that MoveOn and TrueMajority coordinated 1,500 vigils in support of Cindy Sheehan, conservative activ-ist Grover Norquist bluntly warned, "If Iraq is in the rearview

[60] See, for example, David E. Sanger, Michael R. Gordon, and John F. Burns, "Chaos Overran Iraq Plan in '06, Bush Team Says," *New York Times*, January 2, 2007.

mirror in the '06 election, the Republicans will do fine. But if it's still in the windshield, there are problems."[61]

Democratic Caucus Chairman Rahm Emanuel, and former Clinton policy adviser and Democratic Leadership Council (DLC) President Bruce Reed, also displayed something of a phobia toward the antiwar movement. They published *The Plan: Big Ideas for America* in 2006, a five-point platform for winning political power that barely mentioned Iraq, and even then, only evasively (though they did advocate more Special Forces, another 100,000 army recruits, and a domestic counterterrorism force modeled after Britain's MI5).[62] Another book featuring the party's leading lights and edited by Matthew R. Kerbel, *Get This Party Started: How Progressives Can Fight Back and Win*, devoted only two or three paragraphs to Iraq in 200 pages, without calling for an end to the war or offering alternatives.[63] This leadership and consultant hesitation continued throughout 2006.[64]

But the peace movement and the Democratic rank and file weren't having any more of the status quo. While pushing the party leadership toward Murtha's proposal or some kind of exit plan, they began to intervene decisively in the 2006 electoral process from the bottom up.

---

[61] Adam Nagourney and David D. Kirkpatrick, "Bad News Worries Some in GOP on '06," *New York Times*, August 18, 2005.

[62] Rahm Emanuel and Bruce Reed, *The Plan: Big Ideas for America* (PublicAffairs, 2006), p. 56.

[63] Matthew Kerbel, ed., *Get This Party Started: How Progressives Can Fight Back and Win* (Rowman and Littlefield, 2006).

[64] As the *Los Angeles Times'* Janet Hook reported, "Democratic leaders had planned to emphasize domestic policy issues, not Iraq, in the opening weeks of their reign on Capitol Hill . . . Iraq was to be relegated to a strung-out series of oversight hearings. That is, in part, why Sheehan led a small group of protesters to interrupt a news conference on new ethics rules by Representative Rahm Emanuel (D-Ill.) and other House leaders on the first day of the new Congress." See "Democrats Feel Liberals' Anti-War Heat," January 10, 2007.

The Ned Lamont Primary

Several Democratic hawks were confronted with antiwar challengers backed by a new surge of political activism represented by groups like Progressive Democrats of America. The most notable moment was the upset Democratic primary victory of a Dean-style candidate, Ned Lamont, over the pro-war hardliner Joseph Lieberman, who had been the vice-presidential nominee of his party only six years before. Ultimately, Connecticut Republicans backed Lieberman in his November comeback running as an Independent, but the Democratic constituency had issued a definitive mandate for peace.

The activists pursuing nonelectoral strategies weren't sidelined in 2006, but neither did they take off. Some from religious and pacifist traditions sought to promote moral objections to the war through nonviolent civil disobedience. Despite extensive outreach and hundreds of arrests, however, the campaign lacked the scale and fervor of 1960s draft resistance.

Increasingly, activist energy flowed toward breaking the Republican control of Congress. Progressives were active at local political levels (many with anti–Vietnam War experience), presidential primaries were open rather than closed, and, according to opinion polls, the vast majority of the rank and file were antiwar. It was no longer the party of Cold War liberals like Lyndon Johnson.

A typical centrist writer had claimed in the *New Yorker* that the problem of the Democratic Party was its *base*,[65] yet that base was being revitalized by the astonishing energy, organizing, and fundraising of the netroots generation. In the 2006 election cycle, MoveOn, led by twenty-six-year-old Eli

[65] Jeffrey Goldberg, "Letter from Washington," *New Yorker*, January 15, 2007.

Pariser, raised $27 million from its supporters.[66] Those activists poured their support into congressional campaigns.

Few party leaders followed Murtha at first. But antiwar referendums and threats of a primary challenge in her own congressional district helped convince then–minority leader Nancy Pelosi to endorse Murtha's six-month deadline bill. In the Senate, only Russell Feingold had called for a withdrawal deadline, but now John Kerry came around to support a one-year timetable as well. Together, Feingold and Kerry represented a bloc of thirteen Democratic Senators, whose pressure encouraged Senator Carl Levin to advocate the beginning of American troop reductions in six months, though without specifying a timetable for complete withdrawal. His proposal drew over thirty supporters, including Senator Hillary Clinton,[67] thus finally positioning the Democratic establishment as favoring either the beginning of a withdrawal or the actual end of the occupation.

Most significantly, a detailed plan for "phased redeployment" was circulated by the Center for American Progress (CAP), a think tank led by former Clinton Administration chief of staff John Podesta. The plan—for a two-year phased withdrawal—was framed in hawkish terms as a "redeployment" to better position American forces in the war on terror.[68] But it was unmistakably a substantive plan aimed at

[66] Dan Morain, "ActBlue Raises Money Online for Democrats," *Los Angeles Times*, March 11, 2007.

[67] Hillary Clinton was an early and persistent hawk on Iraq, a major factor in deterring many party leaders from taking pro-peace positions. Clinton, however, was pressured by a primary opponent, Jonathan Tasini, in her 2006 New York Senate race, who took seventeen percent of the vote, and she was also booed at a conference of liberal activists in Washington, a foreshadowing of what she might face on the presidential campaign trail. Shortly after the booing incident, she quietly became a coauthor of Levin's plan for the beginning of phased withdrawal.

[68] Lawrence Korb and Brian Katulis, "Strategic Redeployment: A Progressive Plan for Iraq and the Struggle Against Violent Extremists" (Center for Ameri-

158 // ENDING THE WAR IN IRAQ

Democrats and centrists, and was adopted in some form by many party leaders.

I argued that the CAP's redeployment strategy would meet a cool reception, at best, from the peace movement. Indeed, any advocacy of phased or gradual withdrawal, as opposed to "out now," drew angry responses from many in the movement. This was inevitable, I felt, having been in this position many times before. Some activists were left wondering whether they were succeeding or being co-opted. Both readings had some truth, as often happens when grassroots social movements gain majority status. A similar dynamic had arisen, for example, when the Democratic-led Vietnam Moratorium competed with out-now proponents in 1969. My experience told me that these differences needed to be reconciled or they might become paralyzing stumbling blocks.

Many on the left who were committed to third parties or independent mass action as the only way to end the war warned against collaborating with the Democratic Party; one group even declared that the main purpose of their October 2006 demonstration was to "drive home" their criticism of the Democrats. But the "vanguard" was losing connection with the masses.[69]

There was really nothing that could stop this intense flow

can Progress, September 29, 2005); and "Strategic Deployment 2.0: A Progressive Strategy for Iraq" (Center for American Progress, May 2006).

[69] One of the more thoughtful critics of the Democratic establishment was Anthony Arnove, an activist aligned with the International Socialist Organization and author of *Iraq: The Logic of Withdrawal* (New Press, 2006). Arnove, like Mike Davis, complained that the left made a costly mistake in supporting Kerry in 2004, "giving up its independence and principles to support a pro-war candidate" and harboring illusions that the Democrats would become "the standard bearer for the anti-occupation message" (p. 98). Arnove was not all wrong about Kerry, although he ignored the candidate's pointed criticism of Bush's policies as well as their differences on environmental and civil rights issues. Arnove missed the passionate motive of most activists to oust Bush from the White House and deal with President Kerry later. They were lending their energy to the campaign, not surrendering their independence. As for expecting the Democrats to become "the standard bearer for the anti-occupation mes-

of antiwar energy during the 2006 election season. Indeed, there was a *collective logic* in the surge to dump the Bush Republicans in 2006. This was not about morality or ideology but how to most effectively register a blow to the warmakers in the White House. Most Democrats (and even some Independents and Republicans) were convinced by experiences going back to 2000 that ending single-party dominance of the national state was the only way to reverse the war and impact a number of other issues. Seeing no practical alternatives, millions of left-of-center Americans with little confidence in elections threw themselves into congressional campaigns.

In the process of joining this electoral mainstream, the peace movement was in danger of losing its identity. Indeed, there were many forces intent on denying activists any sense of their own agency. Mueller's article in *Foreign Affairs* was only one such example. His conclusion, as previously discussed, was based on a false paradigm of "activism" as consisting only of street barricades and burning draft cards, not taking into account the likes of Cindy Sheehan or Internet activists for Howard Dean.

Another example of discounting the importance of activists came in January 2006, just when congressional opinion was shifting against the war for the first time, one month after the Murtha initiative. A *Washington Post* analysis made multiple references to "public opinion" as a factor in moving Congress, without mentioning any organized lobbying, petitioning, protests, or marches.[70] It was as if public opinion was a magical floating balloon, generated on its own.

My argument is not that an organized antiwar movement was the *only* cause of this shift in attitude, but rather that the

sage," there is no evidence of any such illusion. Ideological opposition to the Democratic Party and mainstream politics tends to blind some critics to certain forms of progress.
[70] Dan Balz, "Tide Turning in GOP Senators' War View; Bipartisan Amendment Is Rebuff to Bush," *Washington Post*, November 16, 2005.

antiwar movement is entitled to claim *some* effect. Otherwise, the millions of leaflets handed out, e-mail barrages to Congress, marches in the streets, sermons delivered, arguments with military recruiters, and simple conversations among neighbors would be defined as having no consequence, and that conclusion would be preposterous.

A better explanation is that it is simply not in the nature of elites (including those within academia and the media) to acknowledge the work of average Americans. Foreign and national security policies are seen as the reserve of the privileged and sophisticated, protected from populist influence. The arbitrary distinction drawn between social movements and electoral activity serves to ignore the former as a driving force in politics. A radical pragmatism might be a better lens for perceiving the dynamics of outside/inside forms of activism.

November 7, 2006: Victory?

On November 7, 2006, American voters caused a seemingly impossible political upheaval by electing Democratic majorities to rule both House and Senate. According to a Gallup poll in August of that year, voters across party lines said that dealing with Iraq should be the president's top priority. For Democrats, Iraq was the top priority among sixty-one percent of voters, with the economy registering second at only nineteen percent; Iraq was first among fifty-two percent of Independents, with the economy at eighteen percent; and among Republicans, the war was on top at thirty-eight percent, as compared with twenty percent for fuel prices and nineteen percent for immigration.[71]

As mentioned earlier, it was the first time in American

[71] Jeffrey M. Jones, "Iraq War Dominates as Americans' Top Priority for Government," Gallup News Service, September 8, 2006.

history that voters in a national election opposed an administration during an ongoing war.[72]

This was a remarkable and unexpected result for a second reason as well: The reapportionment process, in Republican hands, guaranteed safe districts to most incumbents. It was this lock on power, or "duopoly," that had motivated Ralph Nader and the Green Party campaigns of several years earlier. But in this exceptional case, American voters weren't waiting for an independent party so much as wrestling to overturn the reigning oligarchy. Voters who were convinced that the entire system was rigged, or that voting machines were fixed by the Diebold corporation, nevertheless threw themselves against the one-party state. In sufficient numbers, Republicans and Independents joined those Democrats—perhaps for one time only—in throwing out Republican incumbents in their gerrymandered seats, giving new Democratic majorities a year to prove themselves.

The movement could now claim a mandate for peace, leading the ever-hysterical William Kristol to write that "the national Democratic Party has become the puppet of antiwar groups."[73] In late October, candidates had run out-of-Iraq television spots in six of eight contested Senate races and seventeen of thirty-five tight House contests.[74] In a *USA Today*/Gallup survey just before the November election, eighty-two percent of likely voters said they expected a Democratic Congress to set a timetable for withdrawal, and sixty-three percent said they approved of such an approach.[75] Fifty-two percent of vot-

[72] In the 1952 election, voters chose a military hero, General Dwight Eisenhower, to end the Korean War. In 1968, they chose Richard Nixon and his "secret plan for peace" that led to five more years of bloodshed.
[73] Sheryl Gay Stolberg, "A Symbolic Vote Is a Sign of Bitter Debates to Come," *New York Times*, February 17, 2007.
[74] Adam Nagourney and Jim Rutenberg, "Tables Turned on the GOP Over Iraq Issue," *New York Times*, October 19, 2006.
[75] *USA Today*/Gallup poll, October 5, 2006.

ers in another poll supported withdrawal on a fixed timetable, against twenty-six percent who favored the present levels and just twelve percent who wanted more troops in Iraq.[76] Three-quarters of Democrats and a majority of Independents supported the timetable proposal. A December 12 *Washington Post*/ABC News survey was decisive:

- Forty-four percent overall said Iraq was the most important problem to address, as opposed to ten percent who mentioned the economy, five percent who picked immigration, and four percent who answered terrorism.
- Sixty-one percent said the war was not worth fighting, and fifty-two percent opined that the U.S. was losing.
- Seventy-seven percent said the casualties were unacceptable.
- Sixty-nine percent favored "withdrawing almost all U.S. combat forces from Iraq by early 2008, but keeping military training forces there."
- The voters were split on whether to withdraw forces "even if that means civil order is not restored"; however, fifty-two percent said U.S. troops should be decreased, including twenty-eight percent who said it should be done immediately; only seventeen percent favored sending more troops.[77]

There were several other factors at work in the Democrats' victory—general discontent with Bush, congressional scandals, unease about trade agreements, hostility to right-wing Christian hypocrisy—but it was impossible to disguise

[76] *Los Angeles Times*/Bloomberg poll, December 8–11, 2006.
[77] *Washington Post*/ABC News poll, December 12, 2006.

the importance of Iraq to most voters. Ballot initiatives demanding immediate withdrawal passed with eighty percent voter support in Chicago and several other Illinois cities, as they had the previous year in San Francisco and Vermont.

On Iraq, the Democratic leadership had lagged behind the voters for most of the year. Only gradually did House candidates begin taking up the issue, mostly condemning the Bush policies without offering alternatives.

Senator Hillary Clinton, one of the party's leading presidential candidates, was perhaps the anchor preventing the Democratic establishment from following an antiwar platform (before Carl Levin's proposal for troop reductions). It is never easy nor pretty to explore the labyrinth of a great politician's mind, in this case one of the most experienced of the past generation. If I had to guess, it would be that Senator Clinton long ago internalized the idea that Democrats in general, and she in particular, had to retreat from the antiwar sentiments of their McGovernite youths. This approach would only have hardened as the Clintons developed the "third way" politics of the DLC, and eventually succeed in capturing the White House. The line between unacknowledged opportunism and the loudly proclaimed "third way" was impossible to discern, but the Clintons had crossed it with Machiavellian militarism.

The "third way" between the supposed extremes of isolationism and militarism grew to be described as a "muscular internationalism" in which the Democrats would refuse to flinch over the use of force. Never mind that as an air force pilot poor George McGovern had bombed more people during World War II than all the Democratic leaders put together. Soon Madeleine Albright, a friend of Hillary's and the first female secretary of state, was scornfully asking General Colin Powell what all the U.S. troops were for if he wasn't going to use them. After a successful war in the Balkans without American casualties, the Clintons supported regime change in Iraq. Having traveled from McGovernism to muscular internationalism, they were locked into a new delusion. Thinking that supporting the Iraq War would burnish the necessary military credentials needed by a presidential candidate, Hillary Clinton found herself in danger of making the very mistakes that brought the Lyndon Johnson Democrats to ruin in 1968.

In my cynical state, I cannot question a politician's "soul" as I might have long ago. These days I am not sure, theoretically, whether politicians have souls at all. If they do, they need not be reminded. What matters is behavior, which in the case of politicians sometimes requires a repositioning process. Hillary Clinton must now reposition herself on Iraq without appearing to be flip-flopping to cover for a serious mistake. Whether she can do that in the heat of a presidential campaign may determine her future political success.

Former Senator John Edwards chose a different, simpler course for his presidential bid. He admitted that voting to authorize the war was a mistake. There was no backlash against him, only praise, and he had strong support in very early polls.

Another example of the complexity of Democratic antiwar positioning was that of Senator Barack Obama, the most popular speaker on the 2006 campaign trail. Defined in the media as antiwar because of his Chicago speech in 2002 opposing the invasion, Obama's actual stance by 2006 was tuned finely to please peace advocates while avoiding any larger branding. After originally opposing the invasion as "dumb," Obama flew as a senator to Baghdad for thirty-six hours to "figure out just what to do with this mess." There he was mesmerized and "could only marvel at the ability of our government to essentially erect entire cities within hostile territory." He edged toward the phased withdrawal option in 2006, "although how quickly a complete withdrawal can be accomplished is a matter of imperfect judgment based on a series of best guesses," with criteria such as having "some semblance of security." He also wanted guarantees that those in power in Iraq would not be hostile to the U.S. and that the country would not serve as a haven for terrorists.[78] While Obama supporters would call this position "nuanced," it was so calibrated as to be an unreliable indicator of future positions.

Would a President Obama really continue the war if the Baghdad regime was "hostile to the interests of the U.S."? Or would he finesse his way to accepting reality? It is an inherent risk of politics: getting caught between populist voter patterns and the contending counsel of unelected national security elites. On the brink of announcing his presidential campaign in early 2007, Senator Obama settled on a proposal popular with both voters and elites, the Baker-Hamilton goal of removing American combat troops by March 31, 2008.[79]

Another antiwar Democratic candidate, Dennis Kucinich, appeared to have a voice but lacked votes; and deep in the background was Al Gore, perhaps the most electable antiwar politician of all, who seemed to be waiting for an opportunity that would never come.

As the evolving platforms of Clinton, Edwards, and Obama indicate, peace voters can be an important factor in presidential primary campaigns, and sometimes the driving force. Whatever the outcome of the 2008 race, antiwar groups will be factors. Just as politics is too important to be left

[78] Barack Obama, *The Audacity of Hope* (Crown, 2006), pp. 294, 302.
[79] James A. Baker III and Lee H. Hamilton, cochairs, *The Iraq Study Group Report* (Vintage Books, 2006), p. xvi.

to politicians, so is the Democratic Party too important to be left to the Democratic leadership.

Back in Washington, new House Speaker–elect Pelosi sent a message immediately after the 2006 election that she would not "cut off funding" for the war,[80] after previously declaring that impeachment of the president was "off the table."[81] The new Senate majority leader, Harry Reid, speculated that he might even support an increase of troops. Representative Emanuel and other House leaders formulated a six-point, hundred-hour legislative agenda that once again ignored Iraq. It was not as if the jubilant rank and file were expecting immediate withdrawal, but it seemed there was something in the Democratic leadership's blood that froze at the thought of ending the war. They projected an alarming disregard for the peace movement and the campaign workers who had supported them during the election.

The grassroots response was furious and focused, delivered with a paralyzing e-mail barrage to Reid's office. Within days, Democratic leaders were offering reassurances that they had heard the voters in November. Few trusted their words, but increasing numbers of activists were learning the skills of influencing the behavior of their elected leaders. Within weeks, the Democrats cobbled together a rough withdrawal proposal which would serve as their platform heading into the 2008 presidential election season. While it wasn't enough to please most antiwar activists, leaving open the question of whether *all* troops would be withdrawn, it offered a sharp contrast to the Bush Administration's policy thus far. A House-drafted plan called for combat troops to be recalled by December

[80] Alexander Mooney, "Pelosi: Dems Will Not Cut Off Iraq Funding," CNN, January 18, 2007.
[81] Charles Babbington, "Democrats Want to Impeach Bush," *Washington Post*, May 12, 2006.

2007 if the Baghdad regime continued to prove unable to implement necessary reforms. Otherwise, combat troops would be withdrawn no later than August 2008. The Senate, meanwhile, called for all combat troops to be "redeployed" by March 2008. In both scenarios, however, thousands of Americans would remain as "advisers" for years to come.

Attacks in Iraq were at record highs, troops were dying in unacceptable numbers, and voices behind the curtains were worrying that the war was becoming more deadly and unwinnable by the day. Worse, the president was preparing a proposal to send at least 21,500 more troops to Iraq. A potential successor, Senator John McCain, was touring Baghdad with Senator Joseph Lieberman, touting what they called the "surge" proposal. It was fine for the Democrats to pass a flurry of bills on corruption, minimum wage, health care coverage, and oil subsidies, but the elephant in the room was still Iraq, placed there by the Bush Administration.

The established powers were worried.

THE WISE MEN RETURN: THE BAKER-HAMILTON IRAQ STUDY GROUP

No one wants to say it, but the real question is whether the United States can manage to be defeated in Iraq in a way that does not lead to worse disasters in the region—or another terrorist attack at home.

—Evan Thomas, "Iraq Study: Will Bush Listen to Advice?"
Newsweek, December 11, 2006

The report of the Iraq Study Group, chaired by Republican former secretary of state James Baker and the Democratic former House international relations committee chairman Lee

Hamilton, was published the month after the election. Initiated by congressional legislation, the Iraq Study Group was evenly composed of respected senior leaders from both parties. As noted in Chapter 2, the ISG Report, while not wholly welcomed by the peace movement, appeared to be a powerful call for damage-limitation and a face-saving, though partial retreat from Iraq. In Machiavellian terms, it was a sharp retort by the "realists" favoring stability over neoconservative designs for the Middle East.

The Iraq Study Group heralded the return of James Baker—the same Baker who had led the no-holds-barred, some would say *illegal*, effort to secure Florida, and therefore the presidency, for George W. Bush in 2000, earning the bitter distrust of the Democrats. Now Baker seemed to be protecting the system as a whole *from* President Bush. Ironically, the Baker-Hamilton recommendations were becoming the 2007–08 platform of the Democrats.

The ISG Report can be studied as another political positioning exercise, landing at the midpoint between Bush and the pro-withdrawal Democrats. But more than that, it is a blueprint for disengagement, but not necessarily withdrawal, from Iraq through troop redeployments, political negotiation, and diplomacy.

A brutal struggle was breaking out between the embattled Bush White House and the Baker-Hamilton lobby. Behind the scenes, the White House was generating furious pressure against Baker for breaking ranks. In this unfolding conflict, the newly Democratic Congress would adopt the Baker-Hamilton report with a crucial concession to the peace movement: an actual timetable for withdrawal by 2008.

It still is possible that the Baker-Hamilton recommendations can be imposed on Bush. Baker in particular is known for winning his battles. After the 2007 "surge," it is possible that the White House will reverse course, announce the withdrawal of some combat troops, and prepare to fight the 2008 election by stealing the peace issue from the Democrats. But it is more likely that this White House has decided to carry the fight forward and pass the war on to Bush's successors. The politics are shrewd, and put the nation at great risk. If the Bush plan somehow works, he will emerge a winner. If not, he can try to blame the Democrats and the media for losing a war he tried to win. Such a course would contradict the spirit and significance of the November 2006 voter mandate, and perhaps cause a rising confrontation with the antiwar movement in the streets and at the ballot box. It could come to resemble the '60s, when both radical and politically moderate Americans felt enraged at the rejection of the message they felt they had delivered at the ballot box.

The old arguments about social movements versus electoral politics became especially intense as 2007 progressed. On the one hand, the antiwar movement could take credit for shaping the voter opinion that was pushing so many politicians toward antiwar positions. On the other, those politicians were still driven by calculations of interest—not only in their reelection but also in the broader system they now represented. In their electoral districts, they listened to the raw feelings of voters. In Washington, they were initiated into an elite circle that received classified information and briefings from national security experts, in a privileged climate symbolizing the nation's superpower status. They were not likely to take what they perceived to be risky positions for themselves, their party, or their country, if it could be avoided.

For many in the antiwar movement, the behavior of politicians is frustrating and intolerable. The idea of a loophole-ridden one-year timetable—one year for more killing—was too much for many to bear, especially since Bush would veto such a measure. Compromise was unacceptable. *Immediate* withdrawal was necessary, including the withdrawal of *all* troops and contractors, and the closing of American bases. This position, while principled, was doomed.

I had shared this outlook on previous occasions. Even while in the California legislature, I cast more lone *no* votes than anyone in my party, winning few friends in the process. But my studies of, and experiences during, the French and American defeats in Indochina have convinced me that electoral politics play an important role. Without the pressure of social movements and passionate voters, politicians will defer acting for peace. The voters have to threaten the status quo, not simply vote against it. While many politicians will equivocate regardless of public pressure, others can play constructive roles as peace candidates.

The effects of peace politics might include investigating torture accusations, legitimizing dissent, exposing secrecy, restraining escalation, and ultimately end the war. From the 1968 McCarthy and Kennedy campaigns to the 1972 McGovern campaign, from the 1966 Fulbright Vietnam hearings to the 1969–75 efforts to cut off war funding, the Congress was undeniably important in ending the Vietnam War—though always because of public pressure. Yet most writings on Vietnam by antiwar historians belittle or erase the importance of political action.[82] As a result, activists too often confuse the

---

[82] For example, my friend and mentor Howard Zinn argues for an uncompromising moral and disobedient stance against the Iraq War and the establishment as a whole. He asserts an absolute distinction between citizen-led movements and those led by politicians. He has always acted bravely on these beliefs, and I consider him a custodian of our best moral traditions. His historical writings, however, don't give proper credit to the actions of politicians like Bella Abzug, Eugene McCarthy, Robert Kennedy, George McGovern, Frank Church, Mark Hatfield, Mike Gravel, or those in Congress who (however belatedly) voted

nature of political parties with the role of social movements, believing they can put an end to wars "now," or even topple the war-making system in the same process. Such radical possibilities come rarely in American history; and social movements run the danger of underestimating the impact they are actually achieving. America is a better country because of once-radical movements against expansionist wars, slavery, women's inequality, the oppression of labor, discrimination, and pollution. America will be a better country when we withdraw from Iraq. Even so, the U.S. will remain a dangerous Machiavellian nation-state claiming entitlement to a disproportionate share of the world's resources, using and threatening military force, and attempting to limit the expansion of democratic social movements at home and abroad.

Still, ending the Iraq War will be a giant step toward preventing future wars, and will require the combined effort of social movements and political leaders against the very pillars of the policy itself.

to limit or deny war funding. A deeper examination of the complicated relationships between movements and politics needs to be undertaken. Was it the threat of a radicalized public that helped end the war in Vietnam, through, for example, a growing tide of antiwar pressure on the Democratic Party between 1968 and 1972? Or did it end because of the campaigns of a handful of politicians? Perhaps some combination of the two motivated Congress to eventually cut funding for the war; these questions have been little examined. See Howard Zinn, A People's History of the United States (HarperCollins, 2003), p. 498; and Jonathan Neale, A People's History of the Vietnam War (New Press, 2003).

CHAPTER 4

ENDING THE WAR IN IRAQ
RECOMMENDATIONS TO THE ANTIWAR MOVEMENT

A Machiavellian state can neither admit nor accept defeat, for that would undermine its superpower reputation.

Fifty years after its success, the Cuban Revolution has never been recognized by the U.S. The Korean War ended in military stalemate but the U.S. could still claim South Korea as a victory of sorts, and maintain bases and troops there indefinitely.

The Vietnam War ended in the defeat of U.S. objectives, but not exactly a military defeat for American troops. They were withdrawn under the Paris Peace Accords of 1973, and South Vietnam existed for a "decent interval" of two years before falling during an offensive in 1975 without further U.S. intervention.

President Clinton pulled U.S. troops out of Mogadishu, Somalia in 1993 after eighteen Americans were killed in a single day. The U.S. was not technically at war, but the incident was widely seen as a blow to America's status.

The U.S.-led bombing of Serbia lasted for nearly three months until Slobodan Milošević, lacking Soviet assistance, pulled his divisions from Kosovo. Ten years later, the conflict remains unresolved, still the subject of negotiations.

The first President Bush terminated the 1991 Gulf War as soon as he could claim victory and withdraw.

Given such superpower realities, how will the Iraq War ever end?

It might end with an exhausted Balkans-type stalemate and forced partition of Iraq, leaving the U.S. reputation crippled, but with the possibility of bases and oil contracts.

The U.S. could be defeated by the implosion of the Iraqi government and security forces, as happened in South Vietnam.

Those are unlikely scenarios, however, at least at the present.

Two conditions must prevail for the U.S. government to withdraw troops: First, in the minds of American officials, and the elites they listen to, the political, economic, military, and diplomatic costs of the war must increase and the benefits must decline by an overwhelming ratio. Second, a face-saving formula must emerge to facilitate a U.S. willingness to depart. Otherwise, as historian Barbara Tuchman has shown, the "march to folly" will continue.

If the U.S. cannot be persuaded to accept failure in Iraq, the only strategy for ending the war and occupation is to apply people pressure to the following pillars of the Bush Administration's policy:

1. Iraqi Support
2. American Public Opinion
3. American Media
4. Political Support
5. U.S. Military Capacity
6. U.S. Financial Capacity
7. Moral Reputation
8. U.S. Global Alliances

1. The Pillar of Iraqi Support

The U.S. policy of "Iraqization" is a failure. Iraq's security forces cannot possibly defeat an insurgency that the American military has failed to suppress. The notion that Iraqi security forces must stand up before the U.S. can stand down is a delusion that will only perpetuate the occupation. In 2005, the Pentagon's own analysis of the Iraqi forces found that only one of 115 army battalions was "fully capable" of standing on its own; only one-third were deemed "capable" as long as American advisers and air power were provided; two-thirds were "partly capable"; half of all police units were described as "incapable."[1] Little has changed since that time, and Iraqi police units have been described by the *Iraq Study Group Report* as "routinely engage[d] in sectarian violence, including the unnecessary detention, torture, and targeted execution of Sunni Arab civilians."[2]

The Iraqi security forces are an unstable pillar, one on which American policy cannot rest much longer.

Iraqi public opinion is another dimension of this falling pillar. Sixty-one percent of Iraqis now support armed resistance against U.S. troops.[3] Over two-thirds of Iraqis, including both Sunni and Shi'a, support the rapid withdrawal of U.S. troops.

Even the client government is unstable. As of December 2006, 131 of 275 Iraqi parliamentarians favored a deadline for U.S. withdrawal.[4]

---

[1] James Fallows, "Why Iraq Has No Army," *Atlantic Monthly*, December 2005.
[2] James A. Baker III and Lee H. Hamilton, cochairs, *The Iraq Study Group Report* (Vintage Books, 2006), pp. 9–10.
[3] *The Iraq Study Group Report*, p. 35.
[4] Sudarsan Raghavan, "Shiite Clerics' Rivalry Deepens in Fragile Iraq," *Washington Post*, December 21, 2006.

Tasks for Antiwar Activists

Activists can apply pressure on this pillar by demanding that the American media and politicians acknowledge and report on Iraqi public opinion polls. In terms of pressuring Congress, the most broadly supported demand might be to hold hearings on taxpayer funding for Iraqi ministries filled by militias and death squads. Cutting off all congressional funding will be more palatable when people and politicians fully grasp the dysfunctional, repressive, and sectarian nature of the Iraqi government, and realize that American troops are supporting the Shi'a–Kurdish side in a civil war. An alternative proposal would be for the U.S. government to engage the Iraqi opposition, including insurgent groups, to facilitate a popular transitional government that can set a deadline for the U.S. departure in a relatively rapid and orderly way.

2. THE PILLAR OF AMERICAN PUBLIC OPINION

Through late 2006, a fifty-two percent American majority favored setting a short timeline for withdrawal, while they opposed Bush's planned "surge" by a 61-36 margin.[5] There is, however, a fuzzy moderate bloc that believes the war was a mistake but that it might also be another mistake to simply withdraw. The percentage favoring immediate withdrawal has remained fixed at approximately 20-30 percent for two years, while the overall trend has moved away from supporting the war. In partisan terms, nearly three-quarters of Democrats and a slight majority of Independents favor a beginning of withdrawal, while the core of pro-war support is limited to about half of Republicans.

[5] *USA Today*/Gallup poll, January 9, 2007.

Tasks for Antiwar Activists

The primary question is how to move moderate American opinion toward supporting troop pullouts. Every effort should be focused on how best to persuade voters in the middle of the benefits of a withdrawal, without antagonizing them. The key argument to present is that the war wastes lives and neglects other priorities for unachievable goals. Both moderate public opinion and elite opinion can be steadily won using this reasoning. Having a solid exit proposal (see below) enhances the antiwar position. This is a call to cut our losses, which is not the same as "cut and run."

The argument against escalating into Iran builds on the opposition to the Iraq policy. A war with Iran would become an even larger quagmire. Bombing would antagonize the Iranian population, which is three times larger than Iraq. The U.S. lacks the ground forces to occupy the country, and would be hard-pressed to defend against an Iranian ground invasion of Iraq. On the other hand, Iran has real interests in securing a friendly Shi'a state on its border, and in avoiding an overflow of war refugees. Diplomacy offers a better option than escalation.

Until the U.S. announces that it is abandoning the military path, it cannot expect diplomatic and material support from other countries, nor the UN.

As for leaving a haven for al-Qaeda, the U.S. policy has already produced such a result with the invasion, but Iraqi public tolerance of al-Qaeda will probably diminish when American troops leave. Al-Qaeda, Iran, and the Iraqi Shi'a don't share the same political doctrine, and will not likely unite when the Americans leave.

After the Chinese Revolution, American liberals were blamed for "losing China," but Richard Nixon's landmark visit in 1972 paved the way for Jimmy Carter's formal recognition of the country in 1979, and now the U.S. enjoys diplomatic and economic relations, not only with the mainland but with Taiwan as well. When North Vietnam and its allies came to power in South Vietnam in 1975, no new "dominoes" fell. The same dynamic will occur when the U.S. recognizes Cuba.

There is the fear of a repeat of the Cambodia scenario, in which an estimated two million perished at the hands of the Khmer Rouge. Would that happen in Iraq? The comparison is not what it seems. In the case of Cambodia, the U.S. actually accepted the slaughter as the price of its new diplomatic overtures to China, which fully backed the Khmer Rouge. The genocide could have been stopped, as North Vietnam proved by defeating the Cambodian regime in 1979.

If the Iraqi civil war worsens after the U.S. withdraws, the primary responsibility for ending it will lie with the Iraqis and neighboring countries in the region. Having been instrumental in igniting the sectarian strife, the U.S. can offer refugee resettlement, humanitarian assistance, and funds for reconstruction.

These are difficult layers of argument and are not ultimately provable beyond a reasonable doubt. This is why the administration's strategy continues to be based on causing anxiety and uncertainty about the end game, with many Americans wondering if they should just "leave it to the experts."

The antiwar movement, I believe, is a small wheel which can turn the bigger wheel of public opinion, but only when it is properly engaged. This means that working on the fence-sitting voter may be the most important way to end the war. Some will argue that the antiwar movement should "jam the gears" through civil disobedience in order to deliver a wake-up call. The two approaches are not inconsistent, however, as long as the ultimate message is unified. For example, sit-ins at congressional offices of outspoken hawks may be an effective way to interrupt business-as-usual without generating serious antagonism from the public. But the actions will be far more effective if joined to grassroots outreach in congressional districts.

3. THE PILLAR OF THE AMERICAN MEDIA

In 2003, all the major American media were embedded in supporting the invasion. No less than twenty-four national security experts were hired to narrate the invasion to spellbound viewers on ABC, CBS, NBC, CNN, Fox, and PBS.[6] The media therefore bears a heavy responsibility for helping launch the war, and should be held as accountable as any politician or Pentagon bureaucrat. Some outlets, like the *Washington Post* and the *New York Times*, subsequently issued apologies which, however inadequate, are reflective of the importance the media attaches to the potential power of its readers, viewers, and subscribers.

Since 2004, the media has become more critical of the war's progress and the U.S. government's claims, thus expanding and officially legitimizing antiwar sentiment. However, virtually no networks or newspapers have editorialized in favor of U.S. withdrawal, nor presented a timetable (at least not until the Democrats did in early 2007). Nor do they publish the opinions of antiwar critics who favor withdrawal, either in the news or op-ed pages. Even in 2007, as tensions with Iran intensified, the *Times* was congratulating itself for "an admirable search for those likely to have differing views"—but that search was limited to officials from government agencies.[7]

[6] Elizabeth Jensen, "Networks' War Strategy: Enlist Armies of Experts," *Los Angeles Times*, March 18, 2003.
[7] Byron Calame, "Approaching Iran Intelligence with Intelligent Skepticism," *New York Times*, February 25, 2007 (public editor column). Noting that "failing to reach out for dissenting views was a prewar shortcoming," the *Times'* editors asked their military correspondent Michael Gordon to interview the State

Therefore, it is no wonder that forty-five percent of Americans say they "believe little or nothing of what they read in their daily newspapers,"[8] or that millions of Americans now take their news from independent media online, or simply from each other. As a result, the media is an establishment pillar facing a severe legitimacy crisis and audience loss. This provides an opportunity for positive change.

Tasks for Antiwar Activists

It is vital to expand the independent media to all corners of society. This means joining with the vast media reform movement in creating community-based outlets, blogs like DailyKos and *Huffington Post*, and global networks like Pacifica.[9] In the words of Bill Moyers, it means becoming a nation of Tom Paines, each equipped with the technology that can expose and publicize the stories kept marginal by the mainstream media.

The purpose of the independent media goes beyond sustaining a counterculture, important as that may be. It also serves to hold accountable the powerful elites who now command mass-media and politics, gradually forcing attention to alternative information-based realities.

Furthermore, activists can directly approach the mainstream media (just as they make appointments to lobby their elected officials) and demand better Iraq coverage. For example, they can insist on more reporting of Iraqi opinion surveys and inclusion on op-ed pages.

Department in search of skeptical views on Iran's weaponry. That's supposed to be diversity of perspective.
[8] Pew Research Center, cited in Katharine Q. Seelye, "*Times* Panel Proposes Steps to Build Credibility," *New York Times*, May 9, 2005.
[9] Reliable audience statistics are difficult to find for the independent media, but Pacifica's *Democracy Now!* program with Amy Goodman and Juan Gonzales began in 2000 with twenty-five community radio stations, and was broadcasting in 2006 on over 450 radio, public access, and television outlets. Dennis Moynihan, *Democracy Now!*, interview, 2007.

4. The Pillar of Political Support

Bipartisan support for the war has ended. Many neoconservatives are dissociating from the war, following the footsteps of the so-called paleoconservatives (Pat Buchanan, William Buckley, the *National Review*, etc.). There is significant dissent from within the military hierarchy itself. Some Republican officials facing reelection in 2008 have retreated under voter pressure. (This includes Senators like Norm Coleman of Minnesota, Olympia Snowe of Maine, Gordon Smith of Oregon, and John Sununu of New Hampshire, among others.)

The Democratic Party, as a segment of the elite, will never end the war on its own, but its rank and file are a powerful and persistent pressure group. As a result, a majority of Democratic elected officials now favor deadlines either for beginning or completing troop withdrawals. The important change is that one-party control of government has been replaced by critical hearings and debates on the war, thus expanding not only checks-and-balances but public awareness to millions beyond the reach of antiwar groups.

Tasks for Antiwar Activists
An immediate goal will be to isolate and divide President Bush from Republicans by threat of greater political defeat if his administration deepens the quagmire any further. Ten Republican Senators up for reelection are already expressing reservations. One hundred House races, Democratic and Republican, are potentially up for grabs, according to MoveOn.

The antiwar movement should also establish local coalitions to make it as difficult as possible for anyone to be elected president in 2008 without a pledge and a plan to withdraw.

Activists in New Hampshire, Iowa, Nevada, and other early primary states play an important role in pinning down the candidates and sharing what they learn with the electorate.

The corollary of any such approach must be to build links with labor/fair trade coalitions around anti-privatization issues, using Iraq as a foremost example; and with environmental groups fighting global warming, citing Iraq as one of the worst oil-pollution sites in world.

5. THE PILLAR OF U.S. MILITARY CAPACITY

The ISG Report notes that U.S. troops are overextended "to the breaking point."[10] Soldiers are being put through second, third, and fourth deployments, forty percent of them National Guard and reservists. Few U.S. resources are left for other military fronts.[11] Military enlistment is rapidly decreasing, with recruiters struggling to achieve their quotas against community opposition. ROTC recruiters have been forced to withdraw from big northern cities, leaving an army with forty percent of its officers from the South.[12] Captains are leaving the U.S. Army in record numbers.[13] Many governors are signaling that their State Guards are "being stretched" and "putridly inadequate" in terms of equipment.[14] Even military contractors such

[10] *The Iraq Study Group Report,* p. 76.
[11] "Troops and Resources Are Stretching Thin," Center for American Progress, November 29, 2006; "Restoring American Military Power: A Progressive Quadrennial Defense Review," Center for American Progress, January 2006.
[12] "The army's retreat from urban areas has complex roots [including] anti-military sentiment in big cities in the wake of the Vietnam War . . . 'We have leaders in the army who are uncomfortable in big urban areas. They feel awkward there,'" said a former vice chief of staff. Greg Jaffe, "A Retreat from Big Citites Hurts ROTC Recruiting," *Wall Street Journal,* February 22, 2007.
[13] Thom Shanker, "Young Officers Leaving Army at High Rate," *New York Times,* April 10, 2006.
[14] Molly Hennessy-Fiske, "Governors Warn of Troop Buildup's Impact on Guard," *Los Angeles Times,* February 25, 2007. The "putrid" comment was by North Carolina's governor.

as Bechtel began pulling out of Iraq in 2006. Deaths among American contractors are estimated at over 750, though they are not included in official statistics.[15] U.S. death and casualty figures, now about 3,300 and 25,000 respectively, will increase with further combat in Baghdad and al-Anbar province.

The shocking contradiction between the Bush Administration's pseudo-patriotic rhetoric and its budget-slashing and privatizing neoliberalism was revealed in early 2007 in the neglect of wounded veterans at Walter Reed Hospital. Twenty percent of those injured in Iraq have brain injuries which will require lifetime care. The army surgeon-general estimated in 2005 that thirty percent of returning vets would develop mental health problems. The VA's original projection of 25,000 vets seeking medical care had quadrupled by June 2005.[16] Disability claims from depleted uranium can be expected, since more was released in the 2003 bombing of Baghdad than during the first Gulf War.[17] Only after vocal public criticism of Bush's perceived indifference to the injured soldiers at Walter Reed did he visit the hospital, and even then, according to the *New York Times*, the president had reporters tag along with him, "prompting some Democrats and at least one veteran's group to accuse him of staging a photo opportunity."[18]

Most important is the existing as well as the latent opposition to the war within the ranks of the military. Despite an "all-volunteer" army, which was intended to prevent internal

---

[15] Michelle Roberts, "Iraq Contractor Deaths Go Little Noticed," Associated Press, February 23, 2007.

[16] These figures about injured veterans are cited in Linda Bilmes and Joseph E. Stiglitz, "The Economic Costs of the Iraq War: An Appraisal Three Years after the Beginning of the Conflict," National Bureau of Economic Research (Working Paper 12054), February 2006, p. 8.

[17] Bilmes and Stiglitz, p. 10.

[18] Sheryl Gay Stolberg, "Bush Visits the Wounded at Walter Reed Hospital," *New York Times*, March 31, 2007.

mutinies (as happened during Vietnam), the current generation of soldiers holds feelings similar to civilian public opinion. According to a Le Moyne College/Zogby poll in February
2006, seventy-two percent of American troops in Iraq supported withdrawal by the end of the year, including twenty-
nine percent who favored immediate withdrawal.[19] Also in
2006, 1,500 active-duty army soldiers began signing an ap-
peal for redress against the war. Lieutenant Ehren Watada,
the first commissioned officer court-martialed for refusing to
go to Iraq, achieved a mistrial in his February 2007 proceeding
when he insisted on testifying with his reasons for dissent.[20]
These are signs that the military, from bottom to top, is expe-
riencing a deep divide.

Tasks for Antiwar Activists
This crisis helps the antiwar movement argue on behalf of
soldiers. Increased efforts should be devoted to anti–military
recruitment and anti-contractor campaigns. (At L.A.'s
Roosevelt High School, the number of junior ROTC ca-
dets has declined forty-three percent from 286 to 162 since
2003, thanks to vigorous opposition from teachers and parents.[21]) The resumption of a military draft should be firmly
opposed.

Soldiers and military families petitioning against the war
should be identified as potential spokespeople. The message
to soldiers should be that they are being manipulated and coerced to die in vain, or only for each other, not for the good
of the country. The U.S., Canadian, and European peace
movements should support soldiers who speak out, resist

[19] Le Moyne College/Zogby poll, February 28, 2006.
[20] William Yardley, "Mistrial for Officer Who Refused to Go to Iraq," *New York Times*, February 8, 2007.
[21] Sonia Nazario, "Junior ROTC Takes a Hit in LA," *Los Angeles Times*, Febru-
ary 19, 2007.

orders, or seek asylum. In lobbying to cut the funding, the peace movement can nonetheless support apportionments for protective equipment, veterans' benefits, health treatment, and peer counseling (being "antiwar but pro-soldier"). Documentaries like *Arlington West* by Peter Dudar and Sally Marr, and Patricia Foulkrod's *The Ground Truth*, are moving portrayals that should be widely distributed in grassroots circles.

The peace movement should support Representative Henry Waxman's hearings on war profiteering by Halliburton et al, and demand accountability, indictments for fraud, and new policies of dealing directly with Iraqis for reconstruction. Robert Greenwald's documentary *Iraq for Sale* is an excellent tool for outreach, along with Jeremy Scahill's book *Blackwater: The Rise of the World's Most Powerful Mercenary Army* (Nation Books, 2007).

6. THE PILLAR OF U.S. FINANCIAL CAPACITY

Unsustainable short-term budgetary costs of the war are $10 million per hour, $246 million per day, $9 billion per month, and rising. Long-term costs are estimated to be $1 trillion or more.[22] The adverse impact on other funding priorities serves to antagonize key domestic constituencies. For example, the cost of the Iraq War had reached $418.8 billion by April 20, 2007, which could have otherwise paid for 20.3 million four-year college scholarships, or health insurance coverage for 250.8 million kids.[23] Further, tax dollars are being criminally wasted; in 2005, the army paid Halliburton $7 billion in con-

[22] See George S. McGovern and William Roe Polk, "The Way Out of Iraq: A Blueprint for Leaving Iraq Now," *Harper's*, October 2006. Also see Bilmes and Stiglitz.
[23] See Bilmes and Stiglitz. These and other figures are also available from the National Priorities Project at http://www.costofwar.com.

tracts, and an audit found $1 billion spent on "questionable costs."[24]

There are other similar costs to consumers as well; for example, the war has more than doubled the price of crude oil, making U.S. and British oil companies among the most profitable in the world.[25]

Tasks for Antiwar Activists

The peace movement cannot focus simply on decrying violence and government fabrications. It must bring home the costs of war, every day, by using available data from sources like the National Priorities Project to reveal impacts on expenditures for education, health care, housing, and the environment in every state and community. In a red state like Alabama, for example, Iraq had cost taxpayers $3.8 billion by April 2007, which might have paid for 66,496 public school teachers.

For people concerned about homeland security, nearly ten thousand port container inspections could be conducted for the price of one day of the war.[26] Neither the general public nor most public-sector interest groups know of or act on these facts. One significant task is to build coalitions with inner-city, labor, senior, health, education, and environmental groups, along with local officials, and encourage all candidates for public office to refer to these costs of war in their platforms and public presentations. Currently most do not.[27]

---

[24] Griff Witte, "Army to End Expansive, Exclusive Halliburton Deal," *Washington Post*, July 12, 2006.

[25] In 2002, only a single oil company was among the world's ten most profitable corporations. By 2005, four of the top seven were oil and gas companies—ExxonMobil, Chevron, Shell, and British Petroleum. Derrick Z. Jackson, "Big Oil's Bigtime Looting," *Boston Globe*, September 2, 2005.

[26] Senator Ted Kennedy, House-floor speech, October 25, 2005.

[27] In the several Democratic rebuttals to the president's January 10, 2007 speech, for example, there was not a single reference to what the dollars for war might have purchased at home.

7. The Pillar of Moral Reputation

The U.S. cannot sustain itself as a global power if it is hated and drawing suspicion at the levels currently measured in polls. Americans themselves need moral anchoring and respect, and have great difficulty tolerating an image of themselves as torturers and killers of innocent civilians and children. The clergy have not mobilized against this war on the scale that they did in Vietnam. Some Christian evangelicals, including high-ranking Pentagon officials, have introduced an insidious crusader dimension in their denunciations of Allah as a "wicked god," their humiliation of Muslim prisoners, and their rise to leading roles in the chaplaincies of the armed forces. Jewish religious leaders and organizations have been relatively quiet in speaking out, and some have been leading supporters of the war.

The Bush Administration continues to evade congressional and Geneva Convention restrictions on torture and renditions. The U.S. has deliberately understated Iraqi civilian casualties, according to the ISG. The torture of inmates at Abu Ghraib and Guantánamo has been disclosed primarily through leaks and lawsuits, not through government investigations. As a result, America's moral reputation and democratic institutions have been discredited and dishonored, both around the world and inside this country.

Tasks for Antiwar Activists
Restoration of America's moral standing can only be achieved through the deeds of the American people, not the U.S. government, as with the November 2006 voter repudiation of President Bush and his war policies. But individual acts of courage, like the protests of Cindy Sheehan, military families, Iraq War veterans, and active-duty soldiers matter enormously.

America's clergy and people of faith should take the lead in denouncing the immorality of the war, refusing taxes for torture, and countering pro-war stands among Christian and Jewish neoconservatives. Johns Hopkins University's Bloomberg School of Public Health concluded that some 655,000 Iraqi war-related civilian deaths (between March 2003 and July 2006) should be adopted as the most credible evidence of the war's impact.[28] Groups like the ACLU should be supported in their opposition to the Patriot Act, and the new Congress pressured to hold hearings to close all loopholes concerning torture, rendition, repression, and domestic spying.

8. THE PILLAR OF U.S. GLOBAL ALLIANCES

Despite its unilateral posturing, the U.S. needs alliances and global support for the war. That is why the Bush Administration was forced to go to the UN for authorization in the first place, and why it built and touted the "coalition of the willing" when it was unable to secure UN or NATO approval. Now the pillar of international support is rapidly collapsing. The White House's prime ally, U.K. Prime Minister Tony Blair, is widely expected to resign his office in mid-2007, cut British troop levels by 1,600, and promise a full pullout on a 2008 timetable.[29] Two other prime ministers, José María Aznar of Spain and Silvio Berlusconi of Italy, have been driven from office largely over Iraq. The "coalition" provides only a combined 15,000 ground troops, including Britain's 7,000-minus-1,600, far less than the 100,000 private con-

[28] "The Human Cost of the War in Iraq, A Mortality Study, 2002–2006," Bloomberg School of Public Health (Johns Hopkins University), School of Medicine (al-Mustansiriya University) in cooperation with the Center for International Studies (Massachusetts Institute of Technology).
[29] Mary Jordan and Joshua Partlow, "Blair Plans to Withdraw 1,600 Troops from Iraq," Washington Post, February 22, 2007.

tractors, many of them providing military services, on the U.S. payroll.

The *New York Times* placed Blair's withdrawal on page eight, with a headline describing it as only a "trim" when it was really the beginning of a full haircut.[30] One former British defense minister described their army as being on the brink of "operational failure."[31] Only days before, the British prime minister was decrying withdrawals as cowardly strategies of cut and run. The timing was terrible for a White House engaged in sending more troops to Baghdad. It wasn't remotely true that southern Iraq, or Basra in particular, was pacified.

By February 2007, there were only *nine* other countries left with ground troops in Iraq. Besides the U.S. and U.K., the list included South Korea (2,300), Australia (1,450), Romania (1,000), Poland (900), Georgia (850), Denmark (300), El Salvador (380), Bulgaria (153), and the Czech Republic (96).[32] Some sources listed handfuls from Albania, Armenia, Azerbaijan, Bosnia-Herzegovina, Bulgaria, Estonia, Khazakstan, Latvia, Lithuania, Macedonia, Moldova, Mongolia, and Romania.[33] South Korea was reducing its numbers by 800, Denmark by 250, and Poland's troops were all going home by mid-2007.[34] The U.K. pullout was causing Denmark, with 470 troops under British command, to do the same. The British decision also appeared to undercut the commitment of Australia; as the U.K. announced its partial withdrawal, Dick Cheney traveled to Australia to

[30] Alan Cowell, "Britain to Trim Iraq Force by 1,600 in Coming Months," *New York Times*, February 22, 2007.
[31] Kim Murphy, "British Troop Drawdown; Britain Picks Its Battles Carefully; The Military Can't Fight in Iraq and Afghanistan Without Approaching 'Operational Failure,'" *Los Angeles Times*, February 22, 2007.
[32] Murphy, *Los Angeles Times*, February 22, 2007.
[33] Compiled by Global Security at http://www.globalsecurity.org.
[34] Murphy, *Los Angeles Times*, February 22, 2007.

pressure Prime Minister John Howard into maintaining troop levels.[35]

Thirteen other countries had already withdrawn their troops: the Dominican Republic, Honduras, Hungary, Japan, New Zealand, Nicaragua, Norway, Philippines, Portugal, Singapore, Thailand, Tonga, and the Ukraine.

Further, there is no "coalition of the willing" on the economic side, despite Paul Wolfowitz's early claim that Iraq's oil revenues could "really finance its own reconstruction, and relatively soon."[36] International donors originally pledged $13.5 billion for Iraqi reconstruction, but delivered less than $4 billion as the war unraveled; and Saudi Arabia and the Gulf states failed to forgive Iraq's enormous debt.[37]

Few nations in the Middle East are going to give diplomatic succor to the U.S. in Iraq as long as the U.S. continues providing military and financial support to the Israelis in their hardline policies against a viable and independent Palestinian state. Those policies fuel Muslim hatred and distrust of American intentions and diplomacy. The search for Arab support in Iraq is the real reason Bush called for an independent Palestinian state in 2002, but the administration shows no signs of delivering on its rhetorical pledge.

Tasks for Antiwar Activists

Peace groups like London-based Stop the War Coalition are helping to drive the British out of southern Iraq. At this rate, the U.S. may find itself completely isolated in Iraq by the 2008 presidential election. Further, movements in fifteen UN Security Council countries should demand an end of the council's

---

[35] "Vice President Cheney Visits Iraq War Supporter Australia Prime Minister Howard," Associated Press, February 22, 2007.
[36] Paul Wolfowitz, House Appropriations Committee Hearing, March 27, 2003.
[37] *The Iraq Study Group Report*, p. 27.

annual rubber-stamping of the occupation, which must take place by each December.

The Security Council members most vulnerable to public opinion pressures are the U.S., the U.K., France, and maybe even Russia and China. Non-permanent members like Belgium, Italy, South Africa, and perhaps Ghana are also ripe for influence.[38] Links between movements, NGOs, and parliamentarians can be built though the Internet, or by conferences with antiwar groups in other countries, such as the World Social Forum.

A MODEL FOR LOCAL ANTIWAR ORGANIZING

Given a strategy of pressuring these eight pillars, what would an antiwar organizing model look like? The heart of the "pillars strategy" must beat at local levels, among largely volunteer groups like those in Los Angeles neighborhoods who hold peace placards to passing motorists every Friday night. Over four years, these groups have developed a supportive community, educated themselves with readings, speakers, and films, organized phone trees, and taken part in periodic mass demonstrations. Given limits on size and resources, these groups face persistent problems of morale and effectiveness. The pillars strategy can be carried out with a few simple steps:

- set a goal of doubling the active group membership every year, instead of becoming a closed subculture;
- build an ongoing and expanding e-mail alert list;
- develop the capacity to intervene with endorsements, volunteers, and funding in contested political races, including party committee races;

[38] The other non-permanent members for 2007 were the Congo, Indonesia, Panama, Peru, Qatar, and Slovakia.

- work with online groups to publicly oppose pro-war or compromised candidates for office;
- include at least one liaison to every high school and community college campus to oppose military recruiters;
- include a liaison to veterans opposed to the war and veterans' benefits advocates;
- include liaisons to local groups facing budget cutbacks on domestic programs;
- develop the capacity to carry out effective civil disobedience.

The point of these suggestions is for local groups to plant themselves *strategically* where their pressure on the pillars can be effective, without putting unrealistic strains on their own resources. National groups such as UFPJ and MoveOn rest entirely on a volunteer base of local coalitions and political activists. Continuous investment in a grassroots base is the only way to be effective at the national level, in building for mass demonstrations or intervening in political races.

ON SAVING FACE

To my mind, the U.S. government has already "lost face" irretrievably in Iraq, if by "face" we mean honor and reputation. But to withdraw from Iraq, the U.S. government—meaning our national security establishment—will need to salvage what it can in terms of its interests and image as a superpower. The U.S. might withdraw in a sea of blood if the American people do not act decisively.

Some will say that helping our government save face is

not the business of the antiwar movement, and this response is probably justified. In exasperation, I once said to an audience, "They lied to go in, they can lie to get out." But the statement didn't go over, and I realized that many moderate and humane Americans want to consider the consequences of withdrawal before they commit themselves to that solution. Many Americans want to get out of Iraq but they also want an exit plan that minimizes the damage.

Conflict resolution theory requires that adversaries recognize each other's core interests to the extent possible, including reputation and resources, as they seek an end to violence. The Iraqi insurgents, for example, are likely to continue their armed resistance until the Americans explicitly acknowledge their legitimacy, guarantee a timetable for withdrawal, and accept basic conditions for a shift in the political arena, including an amnesty for fighters, the release of detainees, a certainty about shared oil revenues, the restoration of Ba'athist-era officers and professionals, and the avoidance of partitioning the Iraq state.

Further, the insurgents' written platforms and interviews have expressed a willingness to grant concessions to what they consider American interests. The resistance groups have offered contracts to American corporations in the postwar era—with more accountability, of course; and they are open to Western partnerships in their oil development. ("We want to sell our oil, not drink it," is how they typically put the matter.) Both Sunni nationalists and anti-American Shi'a parties separate themselves from al-Qaeda's larger agenda. They may be willing to accept, unhappily, a small contingent of U.S. security forces "over the hill," if not in Iraq itself.

The U.S. has no known negotiating position beyond the demand for dissolving militias and surrendering weapons, offering a token amnesty, and promising reconstruction funds. But these American proposals come at the price of continued and indefinite occupation. It is a policy of negotiating surrender, not negotiating a stalemate.

To facilitate its own face-saving transition, the U.S. could cease suppressing and ignoring the Iraqi opposition. In plain English, the U.S. could do what it does so well—set the CIA loose with bags of money to replace the current Iraqi regime with a transitional one favoring a political accommodation and U.S. withdrawal. In November 2006, National Security Adviser Stephen J. Hadley proposed giving "monetary support" to Iraqi politicians as an incentive to form a new governing coalition.[39] The notion of intervening in Iraq's fledgling political process is hardly new, but so far has not been for purposes of peace.

In fact, the peace scenario proposed here has already been considered and rejected by the White House. In January 2005, the *New York Times* reported:

> One possibility quietly discussed inside the administration is whether the new Iraqi government might ask the United States forces to leave—what one senior State Department official calls "the Philippine option," a reference to when the Philippines asked American forces to pull out a decade ago.
>
> Few officials will talk publicly about that possibility. But in a speech on October 8 [2004], Lieutenant General James T. Conway, who had just completed a tour as commander of all marines in Iraq, said, "I believe there will be elections in Iraq in January, and I suspect very shortly afterward you will start to see a reduction in U.S.

[39] Michael R. Gordon, "U.S. Adviser's Memo Cites Doubt about Iraqi Leadership," *New York Times*, November 29, 2006.

*forces—not because U.S. planners will seek it, rather be-
cause the Iraqis will demand it.*[40]

The argument of this book is that the White House has
deliberately ignored Iraqi (and American) public opinion
since 2003, handpicking and enriching a handful of Iraqi officials willing to go along with the foreign occupation despite
the broad opposition of their own people. What the American government must do, first, is decide whether it wants
to withdraw all its troops on a strict timetable. If so, it must
then take the second step, which is to signal that intent to the
Iraqis, who will form a transitional government to make all
the necessary military, diplomatic, and political arrangements,
including the possible introduction of peacekeeping forces.

During the modest, underreported March 2007 teleconference between several Iraqi peace parliamentarians and a
bipartisan group of U.S. congressional representatives, there
was tremendous support for the words of Shi'a al-Fadhila Party
representative Nadim al-Jabiri: "Putting a timetable on the
withdrawal of U.S. troops is a very important step in giving
Iraqis confidence that the occupation will end."[41]

Instead of shopping with bags of money for a war government, why not shop for a peace government? A nonpolitical
administration of technicians could be employed to restore basic services until new elections are held. A regional or international conference could be convened once the U.S. announces
its plans to withdraw, so that immediate concerns about a
power vacuum or postwar bloodbath might be addressed by
states with stakes in stabilizing the humanitarian crisis spilling

[40] David E. Sanger and Eric Schmitt, "Hot Topic: How U.S. Might Disengage
in Iraq," *New York Times*, January 10, 2005.
[41] Robert Dreyfuss, "Iraq: Pulled Out or Pushed Out," TomPaine.com, March
9, 2007.

over their borders, while also avoiding a regional sectarian war.
The current notion of maintaining tens of thousands of American troops as "trainers" depends on the existence of a viable
nonsectarian Iraqi military to train, an utterly dubious prospect
at this point in time. The option of asking for an alternative
security force, drawn from other countries instead of the U.S.,
should be the decision of a reconstituted Iraqi government.

That's a face-saving plan. Is there a chance the current
administration will accept this advice? Not very likely.[42] But a
future administration might. And if the peace movement and
its political allies want to reach and persuade more ambivalent Americans, proposals such as these might be a good starting point. Granted, an American withdrawal will probably not
happen with the present clique of Iraqis in power in Baghdad.
Waiting for the Green Zone to simply implode and a new government to arise from the embers is irresponsible and unrealistic. Replacement of the current Baghdad regime, withdrawal of
American troops, and international assistance with postwar stability are three interlocked elements of a solution. They are consistent with the peace movement's objectives, while at the same
time offer a face-saving formula for the Machiavellians—under
this president or the next.

ESCALATION INTO IRAN?

If the Vietnam model is followed, the U.S. will escalate the
war to Iran and perhaps Syria in order not to lose. Bush has

---

[42] In desperate times, however, anything is possible. Even former president
Clinton, whose ultimate views on the war are unknown, suggested in 2005,
"We don't want to set a fixed timetable if that led to chaos . . . [But] it seems to
me the best thing to do is to heed the wishes of all the leaders of Iraq . . . who
say they want us to draw down our forces." Robin Wright, "Democrats Find
Iraq Alternative Is Elusive; Party's Elite Differ on How to Shift U.S. Policy,"
Washington Post, December 5, 2005.

already doubled the attack carrier fleet in the Persian Gulf, authorized the killing and capture of Iranian "networks" in Iraq, and mounted a public relations campaign blaming Iran for the manufacture of sophisticated roadside bombs used against American troops.

If American forces are stretched to the breaking point by Iraq, however, where will the ground troops be found for Iran? It is hard to believe that the Bush Administration will order a draft, though nothing should be considered off the table. That leaves aerial bombardment from carriers in the Persian Gulf as the most likely military scenario. If the purpose is to deliver a crippling blow to Iran's modern infrastructure and target their nuclear production facilities, the plan might work, technically, in the short run. But it would marginalize Iranian reformers in a wave of anti-American nationalism, and leave U.S. troops in Iraq dangerously exposed to the possibility of an all-out assault by tens of thousands of Iranian Republican Guards. Southern Iraq and perhaps parts of Baghdad could be occupied by Iran. World opinion could turn sharply against the U.S., even if the bombardment was rationalized as consistent with UN Security Council policies toward Iran's nuclear enrichment program.

The pillars of the Bush Administration's war policy would fall quickly, but it would leave the U.S. in an even more catastrophic quagmire. Few aside from a handful of neoconservatives would support the new war. Politicians with special ties to Israel would support the bombing of alleged nuclear facilities, but be hard-pressed in the extreme to justify the consequences on the ground, where U.S. troops would be sharply disadvantaged, calling up the nightmare of the Chinese army assault on U.S. forces in Korea. The Sunni insurgents and their Arab allies would hardly sit still. In Lebanon, Hezbollah might activate its border conflict with Israel.

Unlike the period 2001–03, there is already a well-argued alternative to another preventive war—the Baker-Hamilton consensus that ample time exists for U.S. diplomatic engagement with Iran (and Syria) before any escalation of hostilities. Thus, from any rational perspective, there is no case for war with Iran. But rationality was never a deterrent in Iraq. It remains to be seen whether the lessons from the Iraq War thus far are discarded on the road to another faith-based escalation.

CHAPTER 5

LESSONS

On March 4, 1953 [shortly before overthrowing the prime minister of Iran], *Eisenhower wondered aloud why it wasn't possible "to get some of the people in these downtrodden countries to like us instead of hating us."*

—Stephen Kinzer[1]

M emories of war will frame whether future wars will be fought or opposed, shaping the choices of coming generations in the United States.

The Bush Administration appears intent on continuing the Iraq War indefinitely, putting responsibility for the outcome—victory, defeat, or civil war—on the next president. This is consistent with the behavior of presidential administrations during the Vietnam War. Democrats in particular fear this scenario, having been blamed by Republicans for "losses" in China, Korea, and Vietnam.[2] Republicans may face setbacks to militarism and unilateralism for years to come.

Many in the media may try to limit the lessons of this war to a list of avoidable mistakes, suggesting, for example, that the U.S. would have won if 235,000 to 500,000 troops (the estimates vary) had been dispatched at the outset. The claim is that larger troop numbers would have stabilized the

---

[1] Stephen Kinzer, *Overthrow: America's Century of Regime Change from Hawaii to Iraq* (Henry Holt, 2006), p. 122.
[2] For a history of this syndrome, see Kevin Baker, "Stabbed in the Back!" *Harper's*, June 2006.

country, prevented an insurgency, and permitted reconstruction. It is a difficult myth to crack, resting on the very super-power assumption—we can do anything with sufficient will and force—which it means to preserve. Even so, there are solid reasons to reject this lesson as fanciful retrospection.

A declassified U.S. military study from 1999 casts doubt on whether even 400,000 troops could have subdued Iraq.[3] There is no reason to believe that more forces would have overwhelmed the obstacles described in this book. First, a resilient Iraqi resistance would have still existed. More troops alone could not have created political stability; but it would have meant more targets for snipers. Regional and global anti-war reaction would have been stronger. These are the reasons the first President Bush didn't send 500,000 troops to occupy Baghdad as the Gulf War drew to a close, saying it would only "show macho" and leave America "an occupying power— America in an Arab land—with no allies at our side. It would have been disastrous."[4] One reason for having a smaller U.S. invasion force was to minimize American casualties, costs, and outcry at home. Previous antiwar movements had limited what the Bush Administration thought was militarily and politically feasible.

Nevertheless, the "more troops" lesson is an easy way to retrospectively salvage the superpower claim, while preventing a deeper examination of U.S. failure. "America's image abroad suffered a blow, but not a fatal one, and in the end, the United States will still be the sole world power," goes this narrative.[5]

[3] Nicholas D. Kristof, "Stumbling around the World," New York Times, January 14, 2007.
[4] Bob Woodward, State of Denial: Bush at War, Part III (Simon & Shuster, 2006), p. 12.
[5] Helene Cooper, "The Best We Can Hope For," New York Times, January 14, 2007.

The lesson of "incompetence" was subscribed to by Kerry Democrats and most journalists. The notion is captured in the title of Peter Galbraith's trenchant 2006 book, *The End of Iraq: How American Incompetence Created a War without End* (Simon & Schuster). But this explanation only goes so far, because it assumes that the invasion and occupation of Iraq could be managed "competently" in a different set of circumstances. Yet the occupation was unwelcome because it overturned Iraqi sovereignty and was perceived as an attack on the Muslim faith, not because bombing and house-to-house searches could have been carried out with more care. It was an unwinnable war not because it was a "dumb war," as Senator Obama has argued, but because it was inherently flawed by a superpower complex and racism.[6] And it was *intentional*, embodying a plan to replace Iraq's state-controlled economy with a privatized corporate one.

Accepting these "lessons" could lead the next generation to look back on the Iraq War as nothing more than the mistaken adventure of an incompetent president surrounded by ideologically driven advisers. The next war, this logic suggests, will be better organized and executed.

But the war in Iraq concerns more than that—far more. It will be the responsibility of the peace movement, war veterans, and the community of sufferers it has created to rescue and debate the *real* lessons. The dead, who are not even counted properly, will die again, this time in memory, if the story of how they were used is not voiced. And the war, after a brief pause, will begin again.

[6] Anne E. Kornblut and Dan Balz, "Clinton Camps Aims to Minimize Differences with Obama on Iraq," *Washington Post*, March 21, 2007.

The Uncensored Lessons of Iraq

Simply ending the war in Iraq, as if it were cutting a business loss, will leave in place the system which led to this catastrophe. By "the system," I do not mean capitalism, imperialism, racism, sexism—the general "isms" that affect everyday existence—so much as the large institutions with vested interests in perpetuating war. Eisenhower called these the "military-industrial complex" in a prophetic speech in 1961. I would refocus the definition to the "military-industrial-and-oil complex"—including contractors like Halliburton, Blackwater USA, and Lockheed, the Pentagon with worldwide bases, the shadow forces of the secret state apparatus, the oil industry and its energy-hungry industrial allies, and the Israel lobby in all its branches. These groups, and to a considerable extent the mainstream media, are vested in maintaining America's vast political and economic reach. What is more troubling, such neoimperial thinking is shared by many Americans who believe their jobs and way of life are protected by America's disproportionate control of the planet's dwindling resources. The fight of the peace movement is not simply against influential interest groups, it is also a struggle to promote consciousness of America's real interests.

Many Americans, even among those who oppose the war, are on some level addicted to the elite's agenda of de facto empire—so long as governance is benign and conducted intelligently. The idea of a multipolar world is discomforting compared to having an alliance of satellites. Even today, the U.S. refuses to relinquish dominance over NATO or withdraw tens of thousands of troops from Germany and South Korea. U.S. bureaucrats are seriously concerned about the prospect of China's military ascendency, while official policy dictates that America is entitled to control foreign oil supplies—by unilateral force, if necessary. No other country enjoys these entitlements.

The war on terror has quickly become a new Cold War. A ubiquitous, undefined terrorist menace replaces the international Communist conspiracy, while jihadists substitute for the godless atheists. Allies are forgiven their shortcomings, even rewarded with political favors, if they lend support to the mission. Domestic programs are sacrificed to the military budget. Even many critics of the Iraq War find themselves arguing that it diverts resources from the "real" war on terrorism, without adequately explaining what such a battle entails.

Meanwhile, the quagmire in Afghanistan is kept out of the public eye. Opium production is tolerated and rationalized to keep Afghan warlords loyal to the antiterror cause. In Colombia, on the other hand, U.S. troops are deployed on the pretext of stopping the drug trade. Like a script of the television show *24* or the recent CIA film *The Good Shepherd*, the war is a shadowy stuggle against hidden enemies, fought with unsavory allies using immoral techniques, said to require an escalation of secrecy in place of democratic principles and institutions. There is no alternative, the public is advised, except a future with more September 11–type attacks, the growth of global extremism, and a loss of resources for the American economy and way of life.

The war on terror is the latest policy framework—following Manifest Destiny, the Monroe Doctrine, the Open Door Policy, the Cold War, etc.—mobilizing Americans against an alien Other and assuming a unique entitlement to projecting power across the globe. The indispensable notion is that we are the indispensable nation.

But the source of our worries should not be the Vietnam

Syndrome or the Iraq Syndrome, so much as the Superpower
Syndrome[7] with its false assumption of a right to dominate in
a zero-sum world.

The war model rests on the dogma that all terrorists,
driven by blood lust against the West, are beyond negotiation
or accommodation. Robert Kaplan's *Warrior Politics* asserts
that cultures which "do not compete well technologically will
produce an inordinate number of warriors [driven] by the
thrill of violence."[8] Samuel P. Huntington's *The Clash of Civilizations*, written at the end of the Cold War, maintains that the
"survival of the West depends on Americans reaffirming their
Western identity and Westerners accepting their civilization as
unique . . . and uniting to preserve it against challenges from
non-Western societies."[9] Huntington worries as well that the
most serious "challenge to America's national identity" comes
from Mexican immigration, linking his global agenda with his
domestic fears.[10] Neatly fitting the same paradigm has been
the wave of neoconservative writing about domestic "natural
born killers" and "super-predators" by James Q. Wilson, William Bennett, and John DiIulio,[11] emphasizing law-and-order
and garrison-state politics after the Cold War.

In these works, *evil* itself appears as the enemy, replacing liberal and social science explanations about the origins
of violence. In Wilson's worldview, for example, there are no

[7] The concept is that of the esteemed Harvard intellectual Robert Jay Lifton,
who directs an important seminar on mass violence. See Lifton, *The Superpower
Syndrome* (Nation Books, 2005). I am indebted also to the work of historian
William Appleman Williams, who analyzed frontier expansionism as the driving force in American culture, serving as the rationale for neglecting domestic
issues. See Williams, *Contours of American History* (W. W. Norton, 1989).
[8] Robert Kaplan, *Warrior Politics: Why Leadership Demands a Pagan Ethos* (Random House, 2001), p. 119.
[9] Samuel P. Huntington, *The Clash of Civilizations and the Remaking of World
Order* (Simon & Schuster, 1996), pp. 20–21.
[10] See Samuel P. Huntington, *Who Are We? The Challenges to America's National
Identity* (Simon & Schuster, 2004).
[11] Kaplan, p. 119.

"operable" causes of violence at all, neither from terrorists nor super-predator gang members.[12] They must all be taken down, without much regard for liberal niceties.

It is instructive to remember that Communism was once defined as inherently evil as well—*godless Communism*, it was called at first, and then the *evil empire*—to justify the Cold War expenditures on nuclear weapons and military bases in every corner of the world. U.S. policy was based on a distinction offered by Reagan's UN ambassador, Jeane Kirkpatrick, between *authoritarian* regimes, those the U.S. supported despite their human rights violations, and *totalitarian* ones, which could not be reformed due to their Communist power structures. When the Soviet regime was overthrown by nonviolent protest, including the actions of its own leader, Mikhail Gorbachev, the theory nevertheless persisted, before reappearing, revitalized, in the war on terrorism.

Labels like *evil*, when applied to Saddam Hussein, Osama bin Laden, al-Qaeda, and others, face a problem of credibility. If they are *incorrigibly* evil, why is it that the United States government conducted so much business with them in past decades? Clearly, on those occasions the evil men were driven by political interests rather than eternal satanic impulses. U.S. officials like Donald Rumsfeld collaborated with Saddam Hussein in the 1980s war against Iran. The CIA, during the Carter years, helped finance and train the Afghan mujahideen.

The great value of good-versus-evil politics is that it jus-

---

[12] In *Thinking About Crime* (Vintage, 1977), Wilson belittles the idea of root causes thusly: "I have yet to see a root cause or to encounter a government program that has successfully attacked it, at least with respect to those social problems that arise out of human volition rather than technological malfunction. But more importantly, the demand for causal solutions is, whether intended or not, a way of deferring any action and criticizing any policy. It is a cast of mind that inevitably detracts attention from those few things that government can do reasonably well and draws attention toward those many things it cannot do at all," p. xv.

tifies never having to negotiate. Who can compromise with evil? Having an evil adversary lessens any internal or international pressure to develop political solutions. When this enemy is defined as al-Qaeda, Hezbollah, or Hamas, there is wider support for military rather than diplomatic handling of conflicts. From a superpower premise, it is simply assumed that military strength can dictate outcomes without political compromise.

But while various individuals or groups might use evil tactics, like unpardonable assaults on civilian targets, it is absurd to think that extremist visions lack political root causes. The 1979 Iranian Revolution was partly a response to the brutal reign of the U.S.-backed Shah. Hezbollah militants emerged from the rubble of the 1982 Israeli invasion of Lebanon. Al-Qaeda was formed in response to the Soviet occupation of Afghanistan and U.S. allegiance to the House of Saud. Denying the political contexts of these extremist groups ignores popular support for their positions, fostering extremism. That is apparently preferable to the wrenching process of readjusting American priorities. Flooding the barrios with police is easier than flooding the barrios with public-works projects. Sending carriers to the Persian Gulf is easier than increasing America's fuel-efficiency. Maintaining foreign occupations is easier than accepting national self-determination. It is only when these approaches go profoundly wrong and end in the loss of American lives that there is a pause to consider alternatives.

We are at a moment for pausing.

More attacks on American citizens, soldiers, and facilities can be expected, not because of an incomprehensible evil, but for reasons once explained by a military leader and former president, Dwight Eisenhower: "Every gun that is made, every warship launched, every rocket fired signifies, in the final sense, a theft from those who hunger and are not fed, those who are cold and are not clothed."[13] When Eisenhower said those famous words, I was just twenty years old. Two years later, John Kennedy declared, "Those who make peaceful revolution impossible make violent revolution inevitable."[14]

At that time, I believed those presidential maxims constituted a sane approach to conducting U.S. policy. Yet today Eisenhower is all but forgotten and the root causes of violence are dismissed as unprovable; in 2003, the American contribution to United Nations antipoverty programs was ten percent of that of the Kennedy Administration.

Americans must learn that the deepest causes of war lie in the actions of our domestic institutions. This is not about "blaming America," but taking responsibility for the role our institutions play in creating the predicaments we face. The imperial projections of entitlement and privilege, the drive for oil and gas, the global arms trade—all led by American interest groups—also result from and perpetuate inequalities and neglected needs at home. It is a vicious cycle: The foreign enemy is used to justify the military buildup and domestic spying, which results in postponing expenditures for health care, housing, and education. The thirst of the oil companies and the Pentagon for free access to energy resources trumps any agenda for sustainable conservation. Cost-overruns in Iraq curtail relief funds for the destruction caused by Hurricane Katrina.

This is not to deny that there are people out there willing to kill American civilians, bomb American facilities, even

---

[13] Cited in Howard Zinn and Anthony Arnove, editors, *Voices of a People's History of the United States* (Seven Stories Press, 2004), p. 512.
[14] Cited in Walter LaFeber, *Inevitable Revolutions: The United States in Central America* (W. W. Norton, 1993), p. 156.

stage another domestic attack. As a resident of Los Angeles and father of a young boy, I worry about these scenarios all the time. I blame the Bush Administration for not making our infrastructure safer by securing ports and power plants. But waging wars in Iraq and Afghanistan (and by proxy in Lebanon and Palestine) will not make my son more secure. Our government expands the pool of future potential "terrorists" every day: Half of Iraq's population is under eighteen, more than two-thirds never attend school regularly, ninety percent view the Americans as occupiers, and at least half are traumatized by the war itself. According to a former U.S. Army captain now working with a Baghdad nonprofit, these children are "ripe for the vengeful appeals of militias and insurgent groups."[15]

I know, therefore, that we live on borrowed time. We can assume that somewhere in our government, plans are already prepared for moving our country in a more authoritarian direction at home and an even more militaristic one abroad should there be another September 11–scale attack. Yet a different future is possible, one based on the premise that Americans have no interest in occupying Muslim lands, shedding Muslim blood, or monopolizing Muslim oil. The vast majority of us are done with the Crusades. Our differences with the bin Ladens of the world are over theocracy, women's rights, anti-Semitism, and environmental pollution, and these can be approached most effectively on the battlefields of civil society. Organizations like NOW, the Sierra Club, and Amnesty International have no battalions with which to invade, only the force of public opinion.

Experts such as Michael Scheuer, who traced bin Laden's commentaries for the CIA, frequently point out that terror-

---

[15] Christian Caryl, "The Next Jihadists: Iraq's Lost Children," *Newsweek*, January 22, 2007.

ists have political platforms which are ignored in the effort to neutralize them. Bin Laden's viewpoint will make many Americans very uncomfortable, but our leaders from John Quincy Adams to Dwight Eisenhower have warned us against risking our democracy and our children's lives in the hunt for monsters abroad. We need strategies for preventive peace, not preemptive war.

Not long after September 11, Scheuer reports bin Laden as having said, "Many people in the West are good and gentle people. I have already said we are not hostile to the United States. We are against the system which makes nations slaves of the United States, or forces them to mortgage their political and economic freedom."[16] Again, in November 2001: "I will ask the American people to check the anti-Muslim policies of their government."[17] And further: "[The American people] had described their government's policy against Vietnam as wrong. They should play the same role now that they played during the Vietnam War. The American people should prevent the killing of Muslims at the hands of their government."[18]

Bin Laden has sounded variations on this theme several times. In April 2004, he wrote the following to the people of Europe:

> *Our actions are but a reaction to yours—your destruction and murder of our people, whether in Afghanistan, Iraq, or Palestine . . . We are both suffering injustice at the hands of your leaders, who send your sons to our countries, de-*

---

[16] Anonymous, *Imperial Hubris: Why the West Is Losing the War on Terror* (Brassey's, 2004), p. 156. "Anonymous" has since been revealed as Michael Scheuer.

[17] Anonymous, p. 157.

[18] Anonymous, p. 157.

spite their objections, to kill and be killed. So it is in the interests of both sides to stop those who shed their people's blood, both on behalf of narrow personal benefits and on behalf of the White House gang. This war is making billions of dollars on behalf of big corporations, whether it be those who manufacture weapons or reconstruction firms like Halliburton and its offshoots and sister companies.[19]

He then made an offer, a

peace proposal, which is essentially a commitment to cease operations against any state that pledges not to attack Muslims or intervene in their affairs . . . This peace can be renewed at the end of a government's term and the beginning of a new one, with the consent of both sides . . . It has been said that a penny spent on prevention is better than a fortune based on cure.[20]

Later, near the peak of the 2004 American election, bin Laden wrote that "your security lies not in the hands of Kerry, Bush, or al-Qaeda. It lies in your own hands, and whichever state does not encroach upon our security thereby ensures its own."[21]

Many Americans will find these words intolerable because of their author. I understand that revulsion. But the struggle for coexistence is with our enemies, not our friends. The U.S. and the Soviet Union coexisted for seven decades. The real question is whether anything is on offer behind the words, or if they only serve as calculated propaganda. Scheuer says that

[19] Bruce Lawrence, editor, *Messages to the World: The Statements of Osama bin Laden* (Verso, 2005), p. 234.
[20] Lawrence, p. 235–6.
[21] Lawrence, p. 244.

there are straightforward demands being made by al-Qaeda for changes in American policy in the following areas, which Americans may want to refuse but should not ignore:

1. U.S. support for policies that "keep Palestinians in the Israelis' thrall";
2. U.S. and Western troops on the Arabian peninsula;
3. the U.S. occupations of Iraq and Afghanistan;
4. U.S. support for Russia, India, and China against their Muslim populations;
5. U.S. pressure on Arab oil producers to keep prices low;
6. U.S. support for apostate, corrupt, and tyrannical Arab governments.[22]

Scheuer properly asks: Where does absolute rejection of all these issues lead? Are there no alternatives? He coolly offers this assessment:

The choice we have is between keeping current policies, which will produce an escalating expenditure of American treasure and blood, or devising new policies, which may, over time, reduce the expenditure of both.[23]

Whatever the risks of different policies, it is certain that old ones won't work. Consider the classic imperial model as depicted by Prime Minister Tony Blair at the height of his own hubris in 2003. As a son of Michigan, I sat in wonder as he said to Congress:

And I know it's hard on America, and in some small corner of this vast country, out in Nevada or Idaho or these

[22] Anonymous, p. 241.
[23] Anonymous, p. 253.

places I've never been to, but always wanted to go. I know
out there there's a guy getting on with his life, perfectly
happily, minding his own business, saying to you, the polit-
ical leaders of this country, "Why me? And why us? And
why America?" And the only answer is, "Because destiny
put you in this place in history, in this moment in time, and
the task is yours to do."[24]

Noble phrasings like these have sent countless young men
into battles for glory. By January 2007, forty-six Americans
from these two states in the "small corners" of America had
given their lives in Iraq, nearly one-third the total for the entire United Kingdom.[25] The estimated $4.98 billion spent by
taxpayers of Idaho and Nevada on Iraq might have paid for
235,000 four-year college scholarships.[26] The questions—*Why*
me? Why us? And why America?—await a better answer than
Blair's rhetorical renewal of Manifest Destiny.

In my experience, peace movements have come and gone,
rarely finding institutional roots when wars finally end. Certainly there are the dedicated Quakers and a handful of scien-
tists firmly opposed to nuclear war, but mass participation in
nonproliferation efforts drops significantly during peacetime.
Peace advocates will have to address more than the virtues of
nonviolence, which they do admirably; in addition, they must
take on the sources of structural violence rooted in American
institutions. Quoting Eisenhower once again, from his fare-
well address to the nation in January 1961:

[24] Transcript, "Tony Blair's Speech to the U.S. Congress," *Guardian* (U.K.), July 18, 2003.
[25] Carol S. Hook and Jill Konieczko, "Iraq Death Rates by State," *U.S. News & World Report*, January 16, 2007.
[26] Figures as of April 20, 2007 from the National Priorities Project (http://www.costofwar.com).

The total influence [of the military-industrial complex]—
*economic, political, even spiritual—is felt in every city, ev-
ery statehouse, every office of the federal government . . .
Our toil, resources, and livelihood are all involved; so is
the very structure of our society.*

Coalitions broader than peaceniks, professors, and angry
vets will be needed for this challenge, and a broader vision too.
The idea held by some on the left, at least historically—that
most Americans are privileged beneficiaries of imperialism—
must be rejected. It is true that Americans, with three percent
of the world's population, consume one-third of the world's
resources, and that must change. But not all Americans have
access to, or consume, those resources equally. For over thirty
years, while the super-rich got richer and the rich aspired to
become super-rich, middle- and working-class incomes have
remained the same in this country, but only because more
family members worked longer hours to make that same in-
come.[27] If racial gaps and gender gaps are closing, it will still
be a century before equality is achieved at the present rate.
Thirty years after the war on poverty was sacrificed to the
war in Vietnam, America's poor are getting poorer once again.
And because of the corporate hunger for cheap labor, and the
hunger of the poor for jobs, the ensuing immigration crisis
is forcing the Third World to rapidly integrate into the First
World.

If this is all that our empire and its permanent war on
terrorism can offer, Americans need to look for a *better life beyond empire.* If the Europeans have adjusted to life after their
empires, have affordable education and health care, enjoy

[27] See, for example, Juliet B. Schor, *The Overworked American: The Unexpected
Decline of Leisure* (Basic Books, 1993).

longer vacations, and live longer than we do, how bad can life beyond empire be? Recent UNICEF–sponsored comparative studies show that the United States and Great Britain are the "worst places to be a child" out of more than twenty developed countries.[28] The U.S. was seventeenth in percentage of children living in poverty, twelfth in education level, and at the bottom in health and safety because of high rates of infant mortality and accidental deaths. The U.S. and U.K. were among the lowest third in five of six categories: material well-being, health, education, relationships, behaviors and risks, and young people's sense of happiness.

We, the American people, are not losing this war, but we are losing as a result of this war. The real losers are George W. Bush, Dick Cheney, Donald Rumsfeld, Condoleezza Rice, and the neoconservatives, who fabricated evidence, exploited public fear, advocated torture and secret renditions, and failed in their efforts to install democracy at gunpoint. They are now trying to attach a patriotic aura to their own mistakes. Since a cycle of blame always follows wars, it is important to take the bloody flag away from the president and his neoconservative friends and understand that *their personal losses will be America's collective gain.*

A neoconservative defeat would mean a triumph for democracy, accountability, civil liberties, and the role of civil society. It would redeem, to an appreciable extent, the moral reputation and standing of the American people in the world. It would be a setback to the architects of such misguided policies.

It could even bring to power, through a future election, a progressive coalition like those of the late 1930s and

---

[28] Maggie Farley, "U.S., Britain Place Last in Child Survey; UNICEF Ranks Well-Being of Youngsters in Developed Countries," *Los Angeles Times*, February 15, 2007.

the mid-1960s. Based on the lessons of Iraq, a new governing coalition could practice diplomacy-based foreign policy, as in some European countries. Following the lead of Brazil, it might impose a tax on global arms sales and redirect the funds to the UN's programs for ending hunger, illiteracy, and water pollution. It could become the leading defender of the Universal Declaration of Human Rights, the legacy of Eleanor Roosevelt. Following appeals from the global south, it could revise trade agreements to protect jobs and the environment, not simply investors and lenders. Acknowledging world opinion, it could join the battle to reduce global warming and finance an energy transition. Toward peace, it could end the undefined war on terror and instead combine serious deterrence with a commitment to engage Muslims politically, starting with the establishment of a two-state solution in Palestine.

The U.S. could positively challenge much of the world, too, on issues as diverse as women's equality, gay rights, freedom of information, banning sweatshops, and revolutionizing the conservation of energy. At home and abroad, a progressive governing coalition might reject the neoliberal view of jobs as a "privilege" and return to New Deal–style promises of full employment and health care. The "free market" model for domestic and foreign policy could be replaced by a progressive pragmatism with goals like those expressed in Robert Kennedy's 1967 speech on the quality of American life, in which he eloquently stated:

The gross national product measures neither our wit nor our courage, neither our wisdom nor our learning, neither our compassion nor our devotion to country. It measures everything, in short, except that which makes life worth-

while; and it can tell us everything about America—except whether we are proud to be Americans.[29]

There is nothing but a lack of vision that prevents us from publishing a quality-of-life index alongside our country's other annual performance indicators, with a requirement that elected officials make measurable progress, say, away from leading the world in arms sales. This may seem the stuff of dreams, but the November 2006 elections showed a powerful mandate, with voters, candidates, and polling groups expressing strong support for exiting Iraq, fair trade, energy independence, political reform, and breaking from the absolutism of the social conservatives. Both parties lagged behind the voter trends.

To prevent war in Iran (or elsewhere, like Venezuela), and to proceed with these progressive transitions, there must be a vast idealistic awakening of the kind that happened, briefly and brightly, in the late 1960s, before it flickered out amidst assassinations too unbearable and reforms too limited.

The reforms of the '60s have nonetheless led to new underlying norms, openings in institutions, and opportunities for globalizing democracy that can inform, energize, and propel social movements to greater possibilities. Perhaps because I have spent the years since 1960 primarily in social movements, as well as nearly two decades in electoral politics, my opinion is that movements are always the point of departure for real change but need to incorporate outside/inside strategies as they grow. It is true that the Machiavellians adjust as well, designing forms of token "participation" that lead nowhere and crafting an electoral system that makes a mockery of participatory democracy. But the Machiavellians are few, and the multitudes are diverse.

[29] Cited in Jack Newfield, *RFK: A Memoir* (Nation Books, 2003), p. 64.

Americans can protest and rebel through many more chan-nels than ever before. The right to know and participate—the core demand of the '60s—has been largely accepted in this so-ciety. It is no accident that the neoconservatives believe that wars like Iraq must be conducted "off camera, so to speak." The greatest threats to the neoconservatives, the Pentagon, the multinational corporations, and the White House come not from caves in faraway countries, but from the gathering force of the American people.